CONT
Loaded with CANDY

OW!

FILLED

H BOX

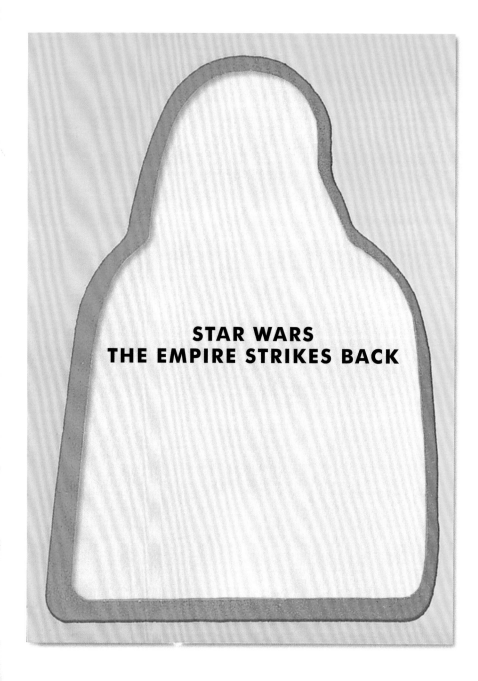

**STAR WARS
THE EMPIRE STRIKES BACK**

THE ORIGINAL TOPPS TRADING CARD SERIES
VOLUME TWO

INTRODUCTION AND COMMENTARY BY GARY GERANI

Abrams ComicArts
New York

TO LEN BROWN OF TOPPS, MY SUPERVISOR, SCI-FI SOULMATE, AND SURROGATE BIG BROTHER

ACKNOWLEDGMENTS: Special thanks to Len Brown and Charles Lippincott, who lived the adventure with me. Thanks also to Ira Friedman at Topps, J. W. Rinzler and Carol Roeder at Lucasfilm, and Harris Toser and Roxanne Toser at *Non-Sport Update*. At Abrams, thanks to Nicole Sclama, Orlando Dos Reis, and Charles Kochman (editorial), Pamela Notarantonio (design), Leily Kleinbard and Michael Clark (managing editorial), and Alison Gervais (production). And thanks to Jonathan Beckerman (photography).

Images courtesy of Robert V. Conte, with assistance from Dave Streicher, from the *Rebuilding Robert Collection*

Photography by Jonathan Beckerman: cover, endpapers, and pages 6, 9, 11–12, 14, 16–17, 19, 198, 382, 514, and 547–48.

Editor: Orlando Dos Reis
Project Manager: Charles Kochman
Designer: Pamela Notarantonio
Managing Editors: Leily Kleinbard & Michael Clark
Production Manager: Alison Gervais

Library of Congress Cataloging-in-Publication Data

Star Wars. The empire strikes back: the original Topps trading card series, volume two / introduction and commentary by Gary Gerani.
  ISBN 978-1-4197-1914-1 (hardcover)
1. Star Wars films—Collectibles. 2. Trading cards. I. Gerani, Gary. II. Topps Chewing Gum, Inc. III. Lucasfilm, Ltd.
  PN1995.9.S695 S8274 2015
  DDC 741.6—dc23
  2015030770

Cover design by Pamela Notarantonio
Case photography by Geoff Spear

Abrams ComicArts books are available at special discounts when purchased in quantity for premiums and promotions as well as fund-raising or educational use. Special editions can also be created to specification. For details, contact specialsales@abramsbooks.com or the address below.

ABRAMS
THE ART OF BOOKS SINCE 1949

115 West 18th Street
New York, NY 10011
www.abramsbooks.com

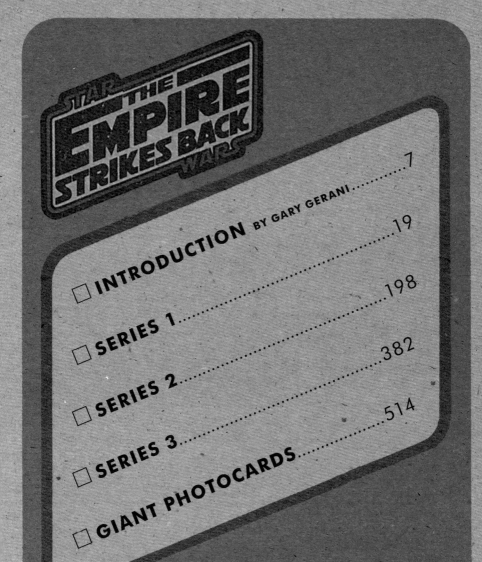

ONCE AGAIN...

TOPPS OFFERS THE MOST EXCITING FORCE IN THE UNIVERSE...

STAR WARS is the NUMBER ONE movie of ALL-TIME. Now, THE EMPIRE STRIKES BACK surpasses STAR WARS with the LARGEST ADVANCE BOOKING in the history of motion pictures.

Last time around Topps sold over a hundred million retail packages of Star Wars Cards and Stickers. Research confirms the same audience — plus many new viewers — are anxiously awaiting this new series of THE EMPIRE STRIKES BACK movie photo cards.

Each pack contains 12 movie photo cards, bubble gum and exciting new Alphabet STICKERS, designed to generate additional purchases. Kids will collect these Alphabet stickers to spell their names or favorite sayings!

Be sure to have adequate back-up supplies in stock to satisfy the tremendous demand for TOPPS' THE EMPIRE STRIKES BACK MOVIE PHOTO CARDS.

THE FORCE IS WITH US . . . AGAIN

25¢

MOVIE
PHOTO
CARDS
BUBBLE
GUM

PLEASE SEND US:

_____ 36-COUNT BOXES OF 25¢ EMPIRE STRIKES BACK
MOVIE PHOTO CARDS BUBBLE GUM. TOPPS # 471

STORE NAME _____

ADDRESS _____

CITY & STATE _____ ZIP _____

AUTHORIZED SIGNATURE _____

PLEASE FILL OUT & RETURN THIS SPECIAL ORDER SHEET TO

topps ®
FOR THE FUN OF IT

A product of Topps Chewing Gum, Inc

INTRODUCTION
THE ADVENTURE CONTINUES . . . AND THIS TIME, IT'S PERSONAL
BY GARY GERANI

It was the ultimate tough act to follow—a challenge even the most resourceful Jedi Knight might find a little daunting. In 1977, *Star Wars* had rapidly evolved from a creative success into a cultural phenomenon, at the time becoming the most successful movie ever made and forging a new pop mythology for audiences everywhere. Sequels were mentioned early on, and the very nature of this swashbuckling spectacle made it ideal for multiple chapters: a big-budget, large-canvas answer to the *Flash Gordon* movie serials that were its inspiration. Amazed, George Lucas was seeing his original vision come to life in a manner far grander and more satisfying than he ever dreamed possible. He set out to create a cool movie for adventure-starved kids and wound up changing the world of pop culture in a way few people anticipated.

That achievement came at a price, however. Physically and emotionally spent after making the first film, Lucas bowed out of helming the second. How, then, would this all-important sequel fare with a different director calling the shots? That question sent tremors through the

Star Wars fan universe. No matter how gifted a replacement director might be, in 1978 the magic touch of George Lucas was considered indispensable. Everyone connected with the project reassured an anxious public that creative integrity would not be sacrificed (usually the case with follow-up films; witness the gradual devolution of *Planet of the Apes* during the 1970s). Lucas would be supervising every aspect of this all-important extension of the franchise, a series with far greater reach than simply that of its moviegoing audience—that's where the magic would start, but if this desperately awaited new chapter fell short, all the merchandising in the world wouldn't compensate for the disappointment.

And disappointment was rampant in the post–*Star Wars* era. Countless imitations of Lucas's brainchild had assaulted viewers since 1977, many of these projects homegrown (such as Glen A. Larson's high-profile television series *Battlestar Galactica*, which boasted impressive special effects from John Dykstra, co-founder of Industrial Light & Magic [ILM] and one of the FX wizards behind *Star Wars*) and some films imported from abroad (such as Roger Corman's release of the Italian space adventure *Starcrash*).

Science fiction in general was enjoying a commercial renaissance due to the one-two punch of *Star Wars* and Steven Spielberg's *Close Encounters of the Third Kind* in 1977. Just two years later, Paramount released *Star Trek: The Motion Picture*, Gene Roddenberry's creation rightfully reclaiming its status as an important sci-fi franchise with a fervent fan base of its own. And even Walt Disney got into the space adventure act in 1979, throwing lots of money and technical expertise into *The Black Hole*, the studio's most ambitious live-action science fiction movie since 1954's Oscar-winning *20,000 Leagues Under the Sea*.

Meanwhile, over at Topps and inside the New Product Development department, things had changed dramatically, at least in terms of my creative responsibilities. From 1972 to 1976, the company's movie and television tie-in projects were notably limited, reflecting America's post-Vietnam and post-Watergate funk. But everything suddenly seemed to go *pop* in 1977, with just about all the shows on ABC-TV's prime-time schedule earning a slew of licensed products, including posters, lunch boxes, and often trading card sets.

And then came that consummate sci-fi blockbuster and cultural game changer: *Star Wars*. In terms of Topps tie-ins, covering the first movie had been a drawn-out process, spread across five trading card sets from 1977 to 1978. Although these sets were and remain cherished by fans, the law of diminishing returns became inevitable as we scrambled to publish every last unit photograph available in the Lucas arsenal, often repeating coverage of key scenes to fill out our needs for each new series.

Still, creating the official *Star Wars* trading cards was reward enough, and we at Topps enjoyed the somewhat giddy feeling that we were riding the crest of a major pop-culture wave of change. After the success of our original *Star Wars* card sets, Topps was on board with the sudden, unprecedented popularity of science fiction subjects on the big and small screens. We kept fans of the genre happy with trading card sets based on *Close Encounters of the Third Kind*, *Superman*, *Alien*, and ABC's *Battlestar Galactica* (although the same network's less-ambitious *Mork & Mindy* proved more profitable).

But all of these variations paled next to the genuine article: George Lucas's irresistible movie galaxy that had taken the world by storm. At some point New Product director Len Brown and I were told the sequel's title, which brought big fanboy smiles to our faces. "I just loved the title when I heard it for the first time," remembers Len. "It was exactly like the old serials, which I grew up with." Indeed, Len and I had tried to revive the classic *Flash Gordon* serial from 1936 as a King Features–licensed photonovel, so swashbuckling space heroes and damsels in distress were very much our cup of java.

TRADING CARD DISPLAY BOX
FOR SERIES 1, 1980.

The first real taste of *The Empire Strikes Back* came in the form of a sneak-peek film clip, which aired on network television in 1979 or early 1980. I happened to be visiting Len at the time, and we made a point of tuning in. The clip showed Han Solo's *Millennium Falcon* dodging asteroids and the laser blasts of Imperial TIE fighters, zooming across the screen and escaping destruction as it sped through the narrow canyons of a giant space rock. This sequence was utterly jaw dropping from beginning to end, more than living up to expectations. "The music!" I remember telling Len breathlessly. Having played the original *Star Wars* album over and over again, I was completely blown away by composer John Williams's brand-new, highly inventive, thoroughly exciting background score.

Topps's higher echelons were paying attention too. "We wanted to do something special for the new *Star Wars* movie," recalls Arthur Shorin, president of the company at the time and final arbiter on all proposed projects. "The first film had hit like a hurricane, and we were determined to repeat or even top ourselves with the sequel," a goal clearly shared by the filmmakers themselves. Reflecting this sense of importance, a decision was made to increase the size of the series: 132 cards in the set as opposed to the usual sixty-six. This would be an epic visual overview worthy of the colossal movie our product was celebrating.

Before very long, I was packing my bags for California again. It had been more than a year since photo needs for the original sets had necessitated a coast-to-coast trip. Since that time, the Star Wars Corporation (SWC) had evolved into something called Black Falcon; now the filmmaker's licensing division was rechristened again, folded into the simple and unambiguous Lucasfilm corporate moniker.

As another indicator of how different things were the second time around, those modest, funky bungalows that housed Lucas's early merchandising operations gave way to an enormous building on Lankershim Boulevard, right beside the Ventura Freeway. Dubbed the "Egg Factory" by employees because of its distinctive crate-like shape, this commanding citadel reflected the seemingly unstoppable power of the still-surging *Star Wars* franchise. Between *The Empire Strikes Back* and *Raiders of the Lost Ark*, George Lucas clearly ruled the pop-cinematic landscape while the rest of us watched in wonderment and anticipation.

Although Charlie Lippincott had left SWC after the first *Star Wars* movie, Carol Wikarska (now Carol Wikarska Titelman) remained a key creative conduit for all of us anxious licensees awaiting visual assets. We were told in advance that a key element of *The Empire Strikes Back* was being

SIDE PANELS FROM TRADING CARD DISPLAY BOXES, 1980.

withheld from publication. Lucas wanted to save this mysterious reveal as a surprise for viewers—a surprise audiences would later talk about in bemused wonder, as they had about the outrageous Cantina creatures from the first movie. This was certainly an intriguing prospect, and we all wondered what the film wizard Lucas had up his imaginative sleeve.

Soon thereafter at the Egg Factory, I was led into a secure room and given a draft of the screenplay to absorb. I remember reading it with much excitement, amazed at the new concepts and characters that

were taking the world's most eagerly awaited sequel into fresh creative territory. Afterward, Carol sat me down in front of a video monitor and showed me footage of the AT-AT walkers advancing on desperate, snowbound rebel heroes. Wow. As a kid who grew up adoring Ray Harryhausen's stop-motion wizardry in movies such as *The Beast From 20,000 Fathoms* and *Jason and the Argonauts*, I was overjoyed to see this technique employed in such a big-budget, high-profile extravaganza. As opposed to dinosaurs or mythological creatures, futuristic metallic behemoths and other

ADVERTISEMENTS ON THE BACK OF CARD WRAPPERS FROM SERIES 1 (TOP), 2 (MIDDLE), AND 3 (BOTTOM).

high-tech fantasies were now being brought to life by stop-animation expert Phil Tippett. It was an exquisite new thrill for fans of the genre, more than worthy of the awe and respect audiences now had for *Star Wars*.

And that wasn't all. What about that "something special" we were told about—the mysterious creative element we couldn't use in our card series (at least initially), but the subject that would have everyone talking? Some top-secret revelation about Luke Skywalker's parentage, perhaps?

Nope. The script I read glossed over the final moments of Luke's heart-wrenching conversation with Darth Vader. The "join me" angle was certainly there, with Vader exhorting Luke to embrace the dark side. But absolutely nothing about . . . well, you know.

At this juncture, I was told that Yoda himself was the creative component Lucas and company wanted to keep secret. The amazing little gnome brought to life by Jim Henson alumnus Frank Oz was not to be featured in any released photos, either in licensed products or publicity tie-ins. He was the Big Surprise, an endearing major character even cooler than the Cantina denizens. Fair enough. There had never been anything quite like Yoda produced for motion pictures, and the brief footage Carol had shared with me was mesmerizing. It wasn't surprising that Lucas, director Irvin Kershner, and the powers that be wanted to keep their scene-stealing new superstar under wraps.

Regardless, I was allowed to select photos with Yoda prominently displayed. I remember being very grateful for that, as this character played a large role in Luke's Jedi training on Dagobah, a key sequence that would have been difficult to cover satisfyingly without having both pupil and teacher in the shot.

With a card count of 132 in the set, we were able to construct a storyboard-like sequence of events, guided by Lucasfilm editors and consultants. The unit photography slide and still coverage was first-rate thanks to George Whitear, whose images would soon become as iconic as similar story-driven photos from the first movie.

I left California with our first series pretty much worked out visually. But I had no idea of a certain plot revelation that my hosts were coyly keeping from me. In other words, the first time I heard that Darth Vader was actually Luke's father was at an official public screening of *The Empire Strikes Back* in Manhattan, several months after our product had been put to bed! Although all of us licensees felt slightly miffed at being left in the dark, this fresh, unrevealed twist gave that first viewing a potent punch none of us who had read the screenplay saw coming.

In addition to the number of card subjects, our *Empire* set boasted something previous *Star Wars* sets never had: a title card. I always felt that a trading card set without a title card seemed undignified, like a book without its cover. Topps agreed

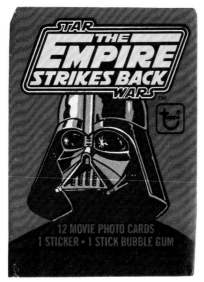

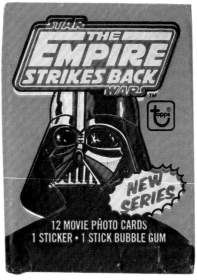

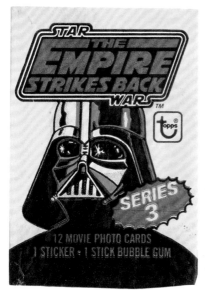

(starting with *Star Trek: The Motion Picture*) and allowed me to run with this approach on all movie- and TV-related products for the next decade and a half. In terms of design, the set boasted a faux-metallic background for its borders and a clean red outline around the picture. The caption, also red, provided a strong statement in capital letters. There was a simple dignity and power to this concept that I always appreciated. We did have some minor problems with a visible cut line (in a few cards, if you look closely, you can see where the "sheets of metal" are joined), but overall our ambitious background treatment was well received at the time.

An equally cool Star File motif was tapped for ten character cards that followed the intro (pages 22–41). Next came the photo-by-photo story line with strong, first-tier image selections that had been worked out with the Lucas editors in California (pages 42–160). Rounding things out was an interesting subset entitled "Space Paintings," which showcased the stunning illustrations that Ralph McQuarrie had created for the film (pages 161–173). These were uncut, "letterboxed" presentations that employed a golden-yellow framing device against that same metallic background, which now took up more of the front space. Years later, Topps would graduate to the elongated Widevision card format to accommodate anamorphically correct images from the Star Wars films, along with production art designed for widescreen.

In terms of editorial copy, I did my best to capture the film's breathless excitement, telling Empire's story card-to-card on backs in a shaped area cannily designed to resemble the film's diagonal logo. Amazingly, Lucasfilm permitted me to write original dialogue for the captions ("Hate me, Luke! Destroy me!" etc.). We even trotted out a wild "coming next" photo graphic for the bottom right corner, a device used most famously in the Mars Attacks set from 1962. And instead of the usual portraits for the set's stickers, we used alphabetic initial graphics (pages 176–186), with photos from the movie contained within each letter. If memory serves, characters were matched to their letters arbitrarily, probably chosen on the basis of how well they fit within a given shape. The backs of these unique stickers featured puzzle pieces that formed a giant photo, a gimmick carried over from our first Star Wars card backs. (Oh, and why in the world didn't we include a full alphabet in this photo-sticker group? That one escapes me completely. Either someone decided it wasn't necessary, or it's another goof-up.) For our box header display, a dramatic line-art portrait of Darth Vader and a simplified version of the portrait adorned the wax wrappers.

Not surprisingly, The Empire Strikes Back (released in the summer of 1980) went through the proverbial roof, both as a movie and as a licensing source for ecstatic kid-product producers. Even before the numbers were in, we were putting Series 2 to bed at Topps, utilizing another 132 images for the card fronts, with additional sticker photos to appear within the alphabet letters. Our front caption and holding line went from red to an equally pleasing blue. For the inevitable Series 3, we changed our silver background color to a faux gold, made the caption and holding line green, and limited our subject count to eighty-eight base set cards and twenty-two stickers (we did not want to repeat the redundancy problem we had back in 1977 and '78).

Our famous trading card items aside, Topps was savvy enough to license Empire for other candy-counter products the company was manufacturing. Plastic

NEWS BULLETIN

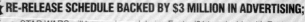

1 RE-RELEASE SCHEDULE BACKED BY $3 MILLION IN ADVERTISING;

a. STAR WARS will be re-released during Easter '81 to coincide with Easter vacations. It will be shown for two weeks in approximately 1,000 theatres throughout the country.

b. THE EMPIRE STRIKES BACK will be re-released between July 31, 1981 and August 6, 1981 to run 4-5 weeks in approximately 1,000 theatres.

c. During the ten weeks of Summer 1982, the two films will be re-released on an alternating basis...One week STAR WARS...One week EMPIRE STRIKES BACK...One week STAR WARS...and so on throughout the summer.

2 AT THE SAME TIME, A TRAILER FOR THE REVENGE OF THE JEDI WILL BE SHOWN;

a. During Christmas 1982, both STAR WARS and THE EMPIRE STRIKES BACK will be re-released to show as a double feature during the Holidays. A trailer for REVENGE OF THE JEDI will be shown at all performances.

b. Burger King will be executing a major promotion program on THE EMPIRE STRIKES BACK in May-June 1981. This is expected to be backed by a multi-million dollar radio and TV advertising program.

c. At least 29 domestic companies are actively producing TESB products. We feel that their activity, along with the promise of "more to come" from LUCASFILM, gives the whole STAR WARS line an enhanced life.

Make sure to keep the following Empire Strikes Back items in stock:
#644 EMPIRE STRIKES BACK CONTAINER HEADS
#492 EMPIRE STRIKES BACK—MOVIE PHOTO CARDS—SERIES 3

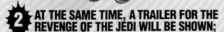

TOPPS RE-RELEASE SELL SHEET, 1981.

GIANT PHOTOCARDS PACKAGE IN ITS DISPLAY BOX.

containers of various character heads were designed in our department and issued early on, including the medical droid and a depressingly short-eared Yoda (given the limitations of injection mold at the time). We also released thirty collectible five-by-seven-inch Photocards of memorable images from the film, with plain white borders and two different sets of backs (pages 514–547). The large format wasn't used again until the Dallas Cowboys Cheerleaders came along in 1981, filling it out appealingly.

The Empire Strikes Back trading card series more than satisfied fans, and various confectionary contributions did the same for avid collectors. Overall, I consider it a better Topps adaptation than our previous *Star Wars* endeavor, partially because of extensive planning and more direct aid from Lucasfilm's better-organized creative staff. The magic hadn't dissipated at all; if anything, interest in that galaxy and its inhabitants from a long time ago and far, far away was greater than ever. Would Han Solo survive his carbon-freeze imprisonment? How would Luke handle the horrific reality of his parentage? And which of our two heroes would Princess Leia eventually choose as the "prince" of her romantic dreams, assuming Captain Solo was rescued? (There was no hint of that sister angle yet, although there were suggestions that feisty Leia was the mysterious "other" Yoda spoke of.)

All of these questions and more would be fully answered in the next episode, *Return of the Jedi*, as Lucas's initial trilogy thundered to its conclusion. But that experience was still two years off. In the meantime, fans got their *Star Wars* fix with the numerous licensed tie-in products conceived by companies such as the one I worked for. We all toiled diligently to capture a piece of *The Empire Strikes Back*'s magic, adding our own special qualities to a franchise that seemed to embrace creativity at every turn. With Yoda blossoming into a full-fledged superstar and everyone talking about poor Luke's unexpected lineage, it was clear that pop culture lightning had struck again for George Lucas—and for the very happy campers at Topps.

GARY GERANI, author of *Star Wars: The Original Topps Trading Card Series, Volume One* and *Star Wars Galaxy: The Original Topps Trading Card Series*, is a screenwriter, author, noted film and TV historian, and children's product developer. He is best known for the Stan Winston–directed horror movie classic *Pumpkinhead*, which he co-wrote; his groundbreaking 1977 nonfiction book *Fantastic Television*; and literally hundreds of trading card sets he's created, edited, and written for the Topps Company since 1972. His graphic novels include *Dinosaurs Attack!* (inspired by his own Topps trading cards) and *Bram Stoker's Death Ship*, an untold story of the Dracula legend. He also has his own publishing unit, Fantastic Press, in partnership with the popular comic book company IDW. Gerani lives in California.

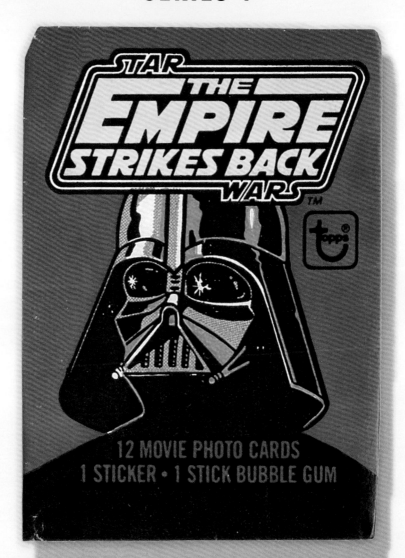

The title card, a recent innovation at Topps, starts off our series. Key art wasn't ready at the time we went to press, so this cool photo of Darth Vader and some stormtroopers was used as an introductory visual. In terms of card back text, the film's concise, serial-inspired opening crawl begins the card series, as it does the movie.

STAR
THE
Empire
STRIKES BACK
WARS™

132 CARDS
33 STICKERS

OFFICIAL DATA

(2) SUBJECT: Luke Skywalker™

CLASSIFICATION: Human
HEIGHT: 5'9"
AGE: 22
EYES: Blue
HAIR: Light Brown
PLANET OF BIRTH: Tatooine
COMMENTS: The son of a famed
Jedi Knight, Luke Skywalker,
star pilot, is currently allied
with Rebel Forces in a battle
against the Empire.
His most noted accomplishment
thus far has been the destruction
of the Death Star battle station.

STAR FILE
OFFICIAL BUSINESS

Luke Skywalker™

We begin our Star File character cards, quite logically, with Luke Skywalker. The design is meant to suggest computer files. There was much concern initially about actor Mark Hamill's appearance following his 1977 auto accident; this bit of reality was worked into the film's opening scenes, where he is mauled by a ferocious wampa. The Official Data backs are concise and quite informative for their day. Notice how we mention that Luke is the son of a famed Jedi Knight. When I wrote this, I had no idea I was referring to Darth Vader, a bit of vital information held back by Lucasfilm, who didn't want to spoil the big reveal.

OFFICIAL DATA

(3)

SUBJECT: Princess Leia Organa™

CLASSIFICATION: Human

HEIGHT: 5' 0"

AGE: 20

EYES: Brown

HAIR: Brown

PLANET OF BIRTH: Alderaan

COMMENTS: A senator and member of the royal family of the now-obliterated planet of Alderaan, Princess Leia continues her work for the Rebellion with the ultimate destruction of the Imperial Alliance as her primary goal.

STAR FILE
OFFICIAL BUSINESS

Princess Leia™

No bones about it, based on my overview: Leia wants the Empire extinguished!

4   SUBJECT: Han Solo™

CLASSIFICATION: Human
HEIGHT: 6' 0"
AGE: 34
EYES: Brown
HAIR: Brown
PLANET OF BIRTH: Unknown
COMMENTS: A former space pirate with a high price on his head, wanted in several star systems by Jabba the Hut. Han Solo is currently working with Princess Leia as a captain in the Rebel forces, following Han Solo's significant contribution to their successful Death Star campaign.

**

STAR FILE
OFFICIAL BUSINESS

Han Solo™

According to these stats, Han Solo is fourteen years older than romantic interest Leia. However, the films never establish the characters' ages.

OFFICIAL DATA

(5) SUBJECT: Chewbacca™

CLASSIFICATION: Wookiee

HEIGHT: 8' 0"

AGE: 200

EYES: Blue

HAIR: Brown

PLANET OF BIRTH: Kazhyyyk

COMMENTS: A Wookiee whose contributions to the Rebellion have earned him the deepest respect, admiration, and honor. Currently Chewie is co-pilot of Han Solo's pirate ship the Millennium Falcon.

STAR FILE
OFFICIAL BUSINESS

Chewbacca™

Blowing up the Death Star earned Chewbacca "the deepest respect, admiration, and honor." But no medal, sorry to say.

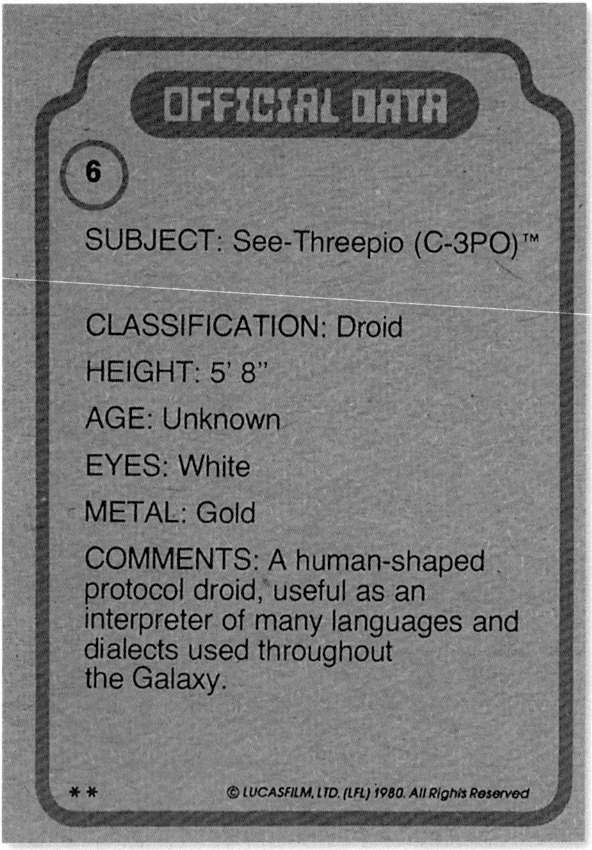

OFFICIAL DATA

6

SUBJECT: See-Threepio (C-3PO)™

CLASSIFICATION: Droid

HEIGHT: 5' 8"

AGE: Unknown

EYES: White

METAL: Gold

COMMENTS: A human-shaped protocol droid, useful as an interpreter of many languages and dialects used throughout the Galaxy.

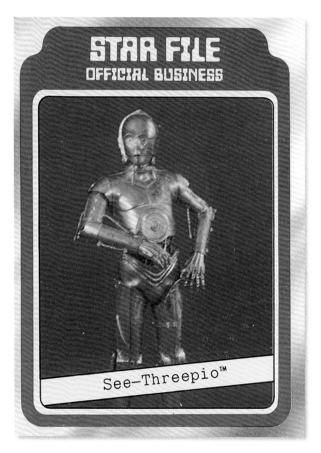

STAR FILE
OFFICIAL BUSINESS

See—Threepio™

I like how the red background of this gallery shot works with our red-outline design scheme. At this point in the *Star Wars* mythos, C-3PO's age is "unknown" (we find out later he was created by young Anakin Skywalker some forty years earlier).

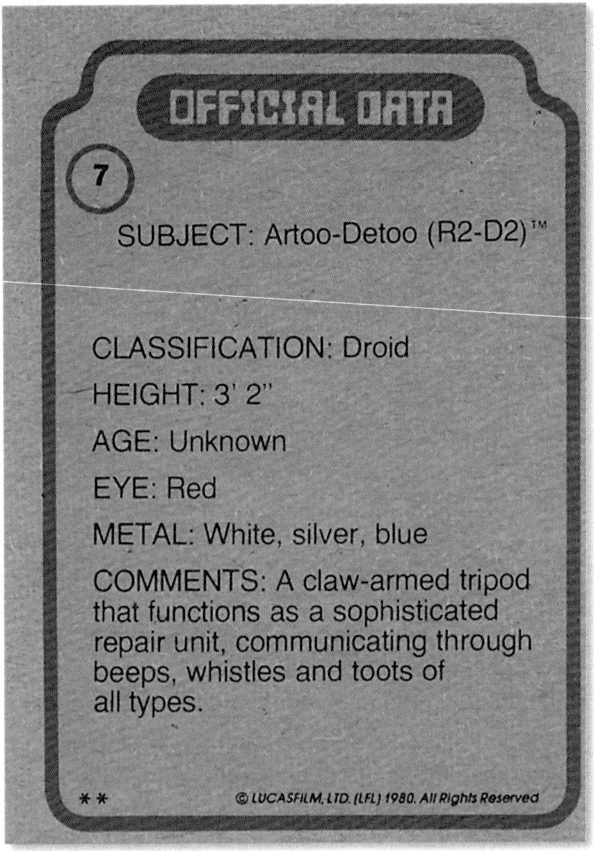

OFFICIAL DATA

7

SUBJECT: Artoo-Detoo (R2-D2)™

CLASSIFICATION: Droid

HEIGHT: 3' 2"

AGE: Unknown

EYE: Red

METAL: White, silver, blue

COMMENTS: A claw-armed tripod that functions as a sophisticated repair unit, communicating through beeps, whistles and toots of all types.

**

© LUCASFILM, LTD. (LFL) 1980. All Rights Reserved

STAR FILE
OFFICIAL BUSINESS

Artoo—Deeto™

R2-D2 was never referred to as an astromech droid (at least not in our card series).

OFFICIAL DATA

8 SUBJECT: Lando Calrissian™

CLASSIFICATION: Human

HEIGHT: 5' 10"

AGE: 36

EYES: Black

HAIR: Black

PLANET OF BIRTH: Unknown

COMMENTS: An ex-smuggler and pirate and once a close friend of Han Solo, Lando Calrissian now runs mining operations on Cloud City of the Bespin system. Cloud City, it should be noted, is a highly technological city whose prosperity stems from the rich resources of Tibanna gas.

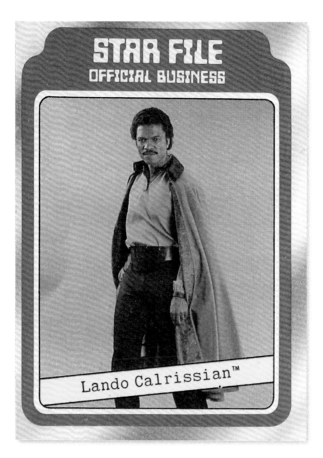

Here's a dashing photo of Lando Calrissian (Billy Dee Williams), the new kid on the galactic block. Notice that Lando is two years older than his gambling buddy Han Solo.

OFFICIAL DATA

(9) SUBJECT: Yoda™

CLASSIFICATION: Unknown
HEIGHT: 2' 2"
AGE: 973
EYES: Greenish Brown
HAIR: White
CURRENT LOCATION: Planet Dagobah
COMMENTS: A teacher, philosopher, and master of the Force, Yoda has instructed many young Jedi Knights by developing their latent physical and intellectual talents. Ben Kenobi once studied under him.

STAR FILE
OFFICIAL BUSINESS

Yoda™

A neutral image was chosen of Yoda on Dagobah, contemplating his new pupil's future. We learn at this early stage that Yoda is an impressive 973 years young according to these stats, though officially we know only that Yoda is more than 900 years old.

OFFICIAL DATA

(10) SUBJECT: Lord Darth Vader™

CLASSIFICATION: Human

HEIGHT: 6' 8"

AGE: 50

EYES: Unknown

HAIR: Unknown

PLANET OF BIRTH: Unknown

COMMENTS: Lord Darth Vader, the Dark Lord of the Sith, is right hand man to the Emperor in all matters and decisions regarding the Imperial Alliance. A former Jedi Knight, he was seduced by the dark side of The Force and has now turned to evil. Severely injured in battle, Vader now requires an elaborate life-support system which is built into his imposing uniform.

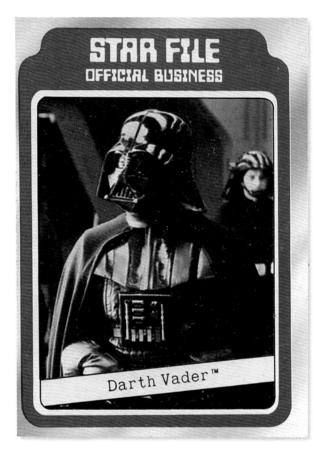

STAR FILE
OFFICIAL BUSINESS

Darth Vader™

Darth Vader's portrait was taken from a scene aboard his personal Star Destroyer, the *Executor*. Again, no hint of his biological relationship to Luke Skywalker in the back text.

OFFICIAL DATA

11   SUBJECT: Boba Fett™

CLASSIFICATION: Human

HEIGHT: 6' 0"   AGE: 43

EYES: Unknown   HAIR: Unknown

PLANET OF BIRTH: Unknown

COMMENTS: The armor-clad Boba Fett is an infamous bounty hunter who has worked with representatives of the Empire before. He is currently being paid by Jabba the Hut to capture and deliver the Rebel captain named Han Solo.

COMING NEXT . . .
Exciting STORY CARDS, beginning with
"The Imperial Probot"

**

STAR FILE

OFFICIAL BUSINESS

Boba Fett™

Aiming for trouble in antiseptic Imperial surroundings, bounty hunter Boba Fett became a superstar before *The Empire Strikes Back* was released, having been showcased in the network TV variety show *Star Wars Holiday Special*, airing November 17, 1978. Notice how we altered the back design slightly to accommodate the "coming next" graphic device, employed for our upcoming story line section.

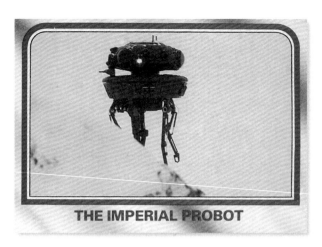

THE IMPERIAL PROBOT

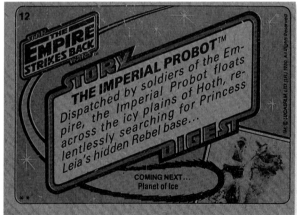

12

STAR EMPIRE STRIKES BACK WARS

STORY

THE IMPERIAL PROBOT™

Dispatched by soldiers of the Empire, the Imperial Probot floats across the icy plains of Hoth, relentlessly searching for Princess Leia's hidden Rebel base...

DIGEST

COMING NEXT...
Planet of Ice

Our Story Digest cards begin just as the movie did, by focusing on the bizarre threat of the Imperial probot.

PLANET OF ICE

13

THE EMPIRE STRIKES BACK

STORY

PLANET OF ICE

Young Luke Skywalker, patrolling the area surrounding the hidden Rebel base, is attacked and thrown from his Tauntaun by a mysterious ice creature. Can the resourceful star warrior survive this unexpected assault?

DIGEST

COMING NEXT...
"Where's Luke?"

Luke is established astride his tauntaun on Hoth. This was one of the first images from *The Empire Strikes Back* released to the public.

"WHERE'S LUKE?"

14

STAR THE EMPIRE STRIKES BACK WARS

STORY

"WHERE'S LUKE™?"

Han Solo strides through Princess Leia's busy military base, glances at Chewbacca working on the Millennium Falcon, then voices concern over his buddy Luke...who is now long overdue.

DIGEST

COMING NEXT...
Droids on Patrol

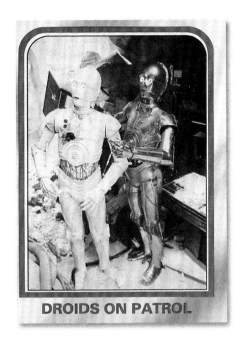

DROIDS ON PATROL

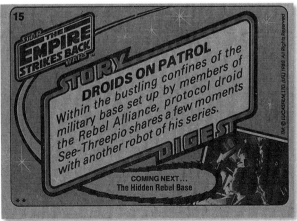

15

STAR WARS THE EMPIRE STRIKES BACK

STORY

DROIDS ON PATROL

Within the bustling confines of the military base set up by members of the Rebel Alliance, protocol droid See-Threepio shares a few moments with another robot of his series.

DIGEST

COMING NEXT...
The Hidden Rebel Base

Nice production shot of C-3PO and a white protocol droid, apparently from a cut scene that would have occurred a little later in the movie. Whitey shows up in a quick cameo before C-3PO makes his appearance, as we get our first good look inside the bustling, Rebel Alliance–operated Echo Base.

THE HIDDEN REBEL BASE

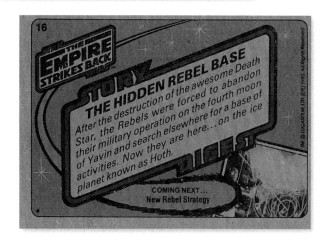

16

STAR WARS THE EMPIRE STRIKES BACK

STORY

THE HIDDEN REBEL BASE

After the destruction of the awesome Death Star, the Rebels were forced to abandon their military operation on the fourth moon of Yavin and search elsewhere for a base of activities. Now they are here... on the ice planet known as Hoth.

COMING NEXT...
New Rebel Strategy

TM © LUCASFILM LTD. (LFL) 1980. All Rights Reserved.

NEW REBEL STRATEGY

17

STAR WARS
THE EMPIRE STRIKES BACK

STORY

NEW REBEL STRATEGY

Against the terrifying might of the Imperial forces, the Rebels must constantly devise new and more ingenius methods of combatting their relentless foes...

DIGEST

COMING NEXT...
General Rieekan

GENERAL RIEEKAN

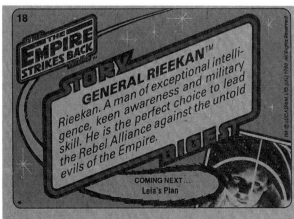

18

STORY

THE EMPIRE STRIKES BACK

GENERAL RIEEKAN™

Rieekan. A man of exceptional intelligence, keen awareness and military skill. He is the perfect choice to lead the Rebel Alliance against the untold evils of the Empire.

DIGEST

COMING NEXT...
Leia's Plan

TM & ©LUCASFILM LTD. (LFL) 1980. All Rights Reserved.

The rebellion's General Rieekan, played by Canadian actor Bruce Boa (*Full Metal Jacket*, *The Omen*, *Superman*), was sufficiently important to warrant his own story card.

LEIA'S PLAN

19

STORY

LEIA'S™ PLAN

The brave young girl whose quick thinking led to the destruction of the Imperial Death Star, Princess Leia Organa continues her tireless struggle against the Empire and its devilish champion, Lord Darth Vader.

DIGEST

COMING NEXT...
Prey of the Wampa

This interesting close-up of Leia establishes the character as a dedicated soldier of freedom, reflected in the back text overview.

20

STAR WARS
THE EMPIRE STRIKES BACK™

STORY

PREY OF THE WAMPA™

Luke, suspended from the ceiling of an ice cave by the rampaging Wampa, manages to free himself from certain doom by using his amazing lightsaber, the weapon first introduced to him by Obi-Wan Kenobi.

DIGEST

COMING NEXT...
Examined: Luke's Tauntaun

PREY OF THE WAMPA

We didn't have images of the ferocious wampa in attack mode, but this view of the captured, upside-down Luke in the creature's ice cave demonstrates its threat.

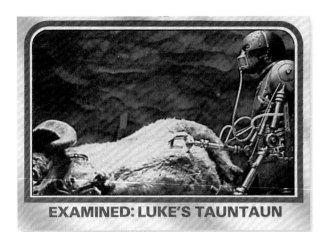

EXAMINED: LUKE'S TAUNTAUN

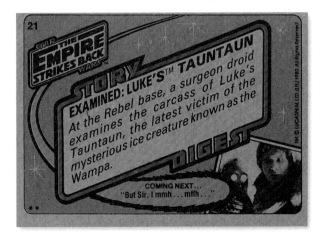

21

STORY

EXAMINED: LUKE'S™ TAUNTAUN
At the Rebel base, a surgeon droid examines the carcass of Luke's Tauntaun, the latest victim of the mysterious ice creature known as the Wampa.

DIGEST

COMING NEXT...
"But Sir, I mmh...mffh..."

In a scene cut from the movie, the carcass of another tauntaun is examined by an Echo Base droid.

"BUT SIR, I MMH . . . MFFH . . . "

22

"BUT SIR, I MMH... MFFH..." An impatient Han Solo decides to set out on his own to rescue Luke. When faithful droid Threepio voices some concern, Solo cuts the conversation short with one persuasive gesture.

COMING NEXT...
In Search of Luke

This fun gesture neatly captures both characters, as Han and C-3PO continue their amusingly tolerant, long-suffering relationship. My dialogue quote for the caption is made up, but it clearly catches the droid's befuddled way of talking.

IN SEARCH OF LUKE

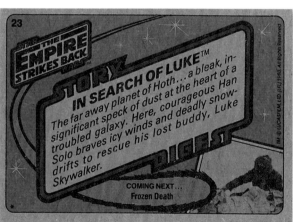

23

STAR THE EMPIRE STRIKES BACK WARS

STORY

IN SEARCH OF LUKE™

The far away planet of Hoth... a bleak, insignificant speck of dust at the heart of a troubled galaxy. Here, courageous Han Solo braves icy winds and deadly snowdrifts to rescue his lost buddy, Luke Skywalker.

DIGEST

COMING NEXT...
Frozen Death

FROZEN DEATH

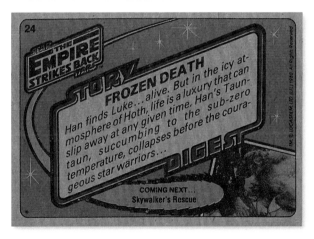

24

STORY

FROZEN DEATH

Han finds Luke... alive. But in the icy atmosphere of Hoth, life is a luxury that can slip away at any given time. Han's Tauntaun, succumbing to the sub-zero temperature, collapses before the courageous star warriors...

DIGEST

COMING NEXT...
Skywalker's Rescue

25

STORY

SKYWALKER'S™ RESCUE

Using the body of the now-dead Tauntaun for warmth, Han and Luke manage to endure the freezing temperature of Hoth before members of the Rebel Alliance arrive on the scene and rescue them.

DIGEST

COMING NEXT...
Luke's Fight for Life

★★

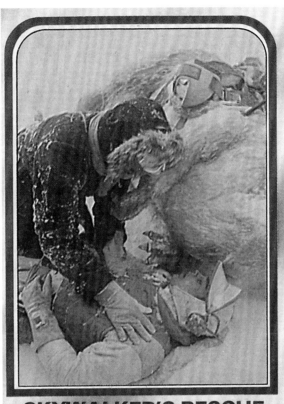

SKYWALKER'S RESCUE

LUKE'S FIGHT FOR LIFE

26

STORY

LUKE'S™ FIGHT FOR LIFE

Only split-second timing and the advanced medical facilities of the Rebel Alliance can save Luke Skywalker's life. Leia and Han watch pensively as their young friend is placed inside the bacta tank...

DIGEST

COMING NEXT...
Rejuvenation Chamber

TM © LUCASFILM LTD. (LFL) 1980. All Rights Reserved.

The first of two bacta tank shots for successive cards. Luke's attack by the wampa and resulting scars were added to the script because of actor Mark Hamill's real-life car accident.

REJUVENATION CHAMBER

27

THE EMPIRE STRIKES BACK

STORY

REJUVENATION CHAMBER

Hours of exposure to freezing temperatures, plus wounds received in his battle with the Wampa have placed the life of young Luke Skywalker in jeopardy. Only the miraculous healing powers of the bacta tank can save him now!

DIGEST

COMING NEXT...
Surgeon Droid

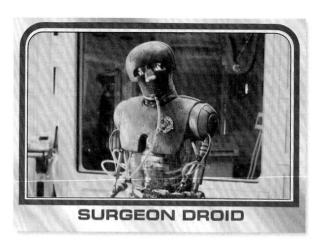

SURGEON DROID

28

STAR WARS THE EMPIRE STRIKES BACK

STORY DIGEST

SURGEON DROID™

Tending the critically-ill Luke Skywalker in the rejuvenation chamber is a surgeon droid, Too-Onebee, one of many such droids designed to nurse ailing humans back to health.

COMING NEXT...
Artoo's Icy Vigil

ARTOO'S ICY VIGIL

29

STORY DIGEST

ARTOO'S™ ICY VIGIL

Artoo-Deeto, the little droid who participated in Luke Skywalker's famous raid on the Death Star, patrols an icy corridor within the Rebel's hidden military base.

COMING NEXT...
Metal Monster

METAL MONSTER

30

STAR THE EMPIRE STRIKES BACK WARS

STORY

METAL MONSTER

Suspecting that something is afoot, Han Solo speeds back into the icy fray along with his companion, the Wookiee Chewbacca. Suddenly, silent scanners focus on the pair. The Imperial Probot has returned!

DIGEST

COMING NEXT...
Zeroing in on Chewie!

TM © LUCASFILM LTD. (LFL) 1980. All Rights Reserved

The Imperial probot's skirmish with Han and Chewie is covered in the next four cards.

ZEROING IN ON CHEWIE!

31

STAR THE EMPIRE STRIKES BACK WARS

STORY

ZEROING IN ON CHEWIE™!

Chewbacca's alarming cry pierces the icy winds of Hoth as the Imperial Probot, its targeting scanners set, closes in for the kill. Where can Han Solo be at this perilous moment?

DIGEST

COMING NEXT...
Han Aims for Action!

HAN AIMS FOR ACTION!

32

STAR WARS THE EMPIRE STRIKES BACK

STORY DIGEST

HAN SOLO™ AIMS FOR ACTION!
Han Solo, a man of action in times of trouble, prepares to deal with the weird-looking Imperial Probot, a sophisticated surveillance device that is now zeroing in on the frantic Chewbacca.

COMING NEXT...
Destroying the Probot

DESTROYING THE PROBOT

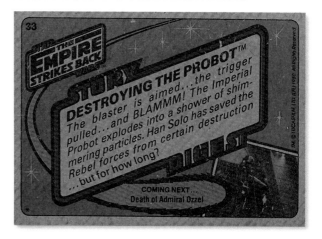

33

STAR THE EMPIRE STRIKES BACK WARS

STORY

DESTROYING THE PROBOT™

The blaster is aimed... the trigger pulled... and BLAMMM! The Imperial Probot explodes into a shower of shimmering particles. Han Solo has saved the Rebel forces from certain destruction ...but for how long?

COMING NEXT...
Death of Admiral Ozzel

34

STAR THE EMPIRE STRIKES BACK WARS ™

STORY DIGEST

DEATH OF ADMIRAL OZZEL ™

Information sent by the Probot before its destruction alerts the Empire's Admiral Ozzel to the whereabouts of the Rebel Base. But Ozzel brings his invading starships out of light speed too quickly... a blunder that costs the portly Admiral his life at the hands of Darth Vader.

COMING NEXT...
The Freedom Fighters

DEATH OF ADMIRAL OZZEL

Admiral Ozzel's demise enabled us to introduce Darth Vader into our trading card story line with a melodramatic flourish, the vertical image adding to his awesomeness.

THE FREEDOM FIGHTERS

35

STAR WARS THE EMPIRE STRIKES BACK

STORY

THE FREEDOM FIGHTERS

The Rebels have discovered that warships from the Empire are on their way to Hoth. Instantly, they race to their X-wing fighters and prepare for a major confrontation...

DIGEST

COMING NEXT...
Rebel Defenses

REBEL DEFENSES

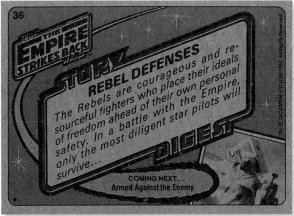

36

THE EMPIRE STRIKES BACK™

STORY

REBEL DEFENSES
The Rebels are courageous and re-sourceful fighters who place their ideals of freedom ahead of their own personal safety. In a battle with the Empire, only the most diligent star pilots will survive...

DIGEST

COMING NEXT...
Armed Against the Enemy

The saga's fanciful, futuristic weaponry and hardware are given a different psychological spin when transferred to the bleak, snowbound environment of Hoth.

ARMED AGAINST THE ENEMY

37

THE
EMPIRE
STRIKES BACK

STORY

ARMED AGAINST THE ENEMY

Although the Rebel forces are well-armed, no one denies that the Empire is a far more powerful adversary. Lord Vader and his cronies have plundered the riches of a thousand worlds to bolster their ever-growing armies.

COMING NEXT...
Joined by Dack

JOINED BY DACK

38

STORY

JOINED BY DACK™

Dack, a young Rebel pilot, teams up with Luke Skywalker in his snow-speeder as a major battle between Rebel forces and the Imperial Alliance begins to take shape!

DIGEST

COMING NEXT...
The Sound of Terror

Dack's last name is Ralter, and he was played by actor and stuntman John Morton. Morton also body-doubled for Boba Fett and appeared in *Superman II* and Dino De Laurentiis's *Flash Gordon*. Although "Dack's" name was approved as you see it on this card, it is officially spelled Dak in the current *Star Wars* canon.

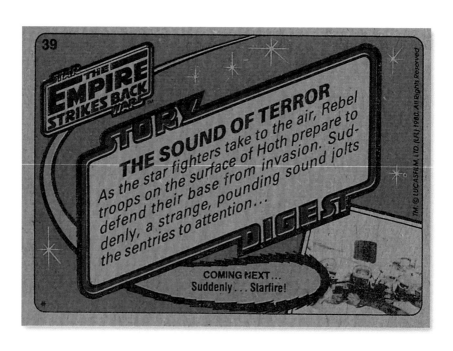

39

THE EMPIRE STRIKES BACK

STORY

THE SOUND OF TERROR

As the star fighters take to the air, Rebel troops on the surface of Hoth prepare to defend their base from invasion. Suddenly, a strange, pounding sound jolts the sentries to attention...

DIGEST

COMING NEXT...
Suddenly... Starfire!

THE SOUND OF TERROR

SUDDENLY . . . STARFIRE!

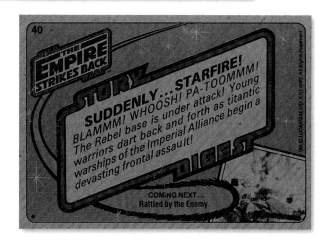

40

STAR WARS
THE EMPIRE STRIKES BACK

STORY DIGEST

SUDDENLY . . . STARFIRE!
BLAMMM! WHOOSH! PA-TOOMMM!
The Rebel base is under attack! Young
warriors dart back and forth as titantic
warships of the Imperial Alliance begin a
devasting frontal assault!

COMING NEXT...
Rattled by the Enemy

RATTLED BY THE ENEMY

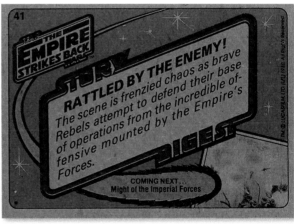

41

THE EMPIRE STRIKES BACK

STORY

RATTLED BY THE ENEMY!

The scene is frenzied chaos as brave Rebels attempt to defend their base of operations from the incredible offensive mounted by the Empire's Forces.

DIGEST

COMING NEXT...
Might of the Imperial Forces

MIGHT OF THE IMPERIAL FORCES

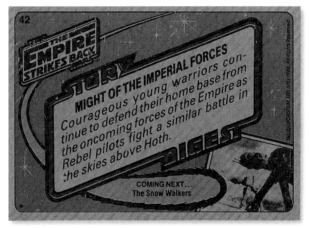

42

STORY

MIGHT OF THE IMPERIAL FORCES

Courageous young warriors continue to defend their home base from the oncoming forces of the Empire as Rebel pilots fight a similar battle in the skies above Hoth.

DIGEST

COMING NEXT...
The Snow Walkers

THE SNOW WALKERS™

43

STORY

THE SNOW WALKERS™

Instrumental in the major offensive launched by the Empire are the Imperial snow walkers, giant behemoth machines that crush all obstacles in their path. What chance does the Rebel Alliance have against weapons such as these?

DIGEST

COMING NEXT...
Luke . . . Trapped!

After several cards showing rebel forces under attack, we finally reveal what is pouring it on: the Imperial snow walkers, which are never identified in this set as AT-ATs. This airbrushed beauty is clearly our money shot for the first series.

LUKE . . . TRAPPED!

STORY

LUKE™ . . . TRAPPED!

Luke Skywalker, crashed on the surface of Hoth with his co-pilot Dack, tries desperately to push his way out of the cockpit before an Imperial snow walker crushes his vehicle into flattened metal.

DIGEST

COMING NEXT...
Escape from Icy Peril!

ESCAPE FROM ICY PERIL

45

STORY

ESCAPE FROM ICY PERIL

Dack, Luke's friend and co-pilot, is dead. Now Luke uses all of his skill and ingenuity to cut a hole in the bottom of the deadly snow walker, plant a special grenade inside, and roll to safety as the metal monster explodes into luminous particles.

DIGEST

COMING NEXT...
"Retreat! Retreat!"

" RETREAT! RETREAT!"

Here's a moody, evocative full shot of rebels in retreat on Hoth.

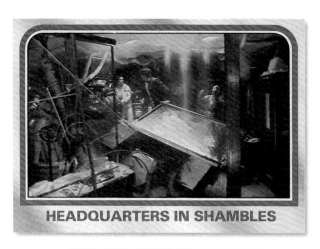

HEADQUARTERS IN SHAMBLES

47

STAR THE EMPIRE STRIKES BACK STAR

STORY

HEADQUARTERS IN SHAMBLES

The remaining members of the Rebel Alliance scramble for cover as their once secure base crumbles all about them. Valuable plans and tactical information are whisked away before the icy walls cave in...

COMING NEXT...
Solo's Makeshift Escape

SOLO'S MAKESHIFT ESCAPE

INVADED!

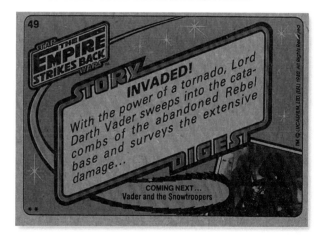

49

STAR WARS THE EMPIRE STRIKES BACK

STORY

INVADED!
With the power of a tornado, Lord Darth Vader sweeps into the cata-combs of the abandoned Rebel base and surveys the extensive damage...

DIGEST

COMING NEXT...
Vader and the Snowtroopers

VADER AND THE SNOWTROOPERS

50

EMPIRE STRIKES BACK

STORY

VADER AND THE SNOWTROOPERS™
Darth Vader, the Dark Lord of the Sith, stalks the excavated ice caves that once housed the headquarters of the Rebel movement...

COMING NEXT...
Snowtroopers of the Empire

SNOWTROOPERS OF THE EMPIRE

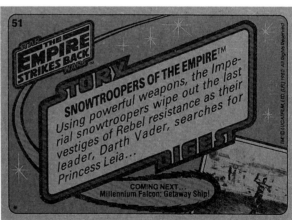

51

STAR WARS THE EMPIRE STRIKES BACK

STORY DIGEST

SNOWTROOPERS OF THE EMPIRE™

Using powerful weapons, the Imperial snowtroopers wipe out the last vestiges of Rebel resistance as their leader, Darth Vader, searches for Princess Leia…

COMING NEXT…
Millennium Falcon: Getaway Ship!

MILLENNIUM FALCON: GETAWAY SHIP!

52

STORY

MILLENNIUM FALCON™: GETAWAY SHIP!
"Wait for me, Sir!" shouts See-Threepio as Han Solo, Chewbacca and Princess Leia scramble into the Millennium Falcon for an emergency launch.

DIGEST

COMING NEXT...
Emergency Blast Off!

EMERGENCY BLAST OFF!

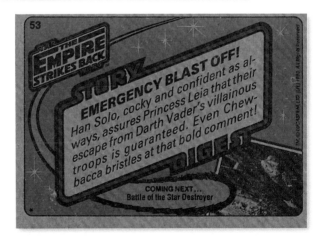

53

STAR THE **EMPIRE** STRIKES BACK WARS

STORY

EMERGENCY BLAST OFF!
Han Solo, cocky and confident as always, assures Princess Leia that their
escape from Darth Vader's villainous
troops is guaranteed. Even Chewbacca bristles at that bold comment!

COMING NEXT...
Battle of the Star Destroyer

This card nicely captures Han Solo's humorous uncertainty and reflexive bravado as he and his rescued pals try to navigate past the Empire's eager clutches.

BATTLE OF THE STAR DESTROYER

54

STAR THE **EMPIRE** STRIKES BACK WARS

STORY

BATTLE OF THE STAR DESTROYER™

Teeth gritted, space privateer Han Solo displays his combat skills as he guides the Millennium Falcon through a hazardous cat-and-mouse chase with an Imperial Star Destroyer!

DIGEST

COMING NEXT...
Fix-it Man Han Solo!

TM © LUCASFILM LTD. (LFL) 1980. All Rights Reserved

Another spectacular money shot, carefully prepared by Lucasfilm and ILM. This one tracks the *Millennium Falcon*'s wild flight as it dodges Imperial laser blasts while being pursued by Vader's imposing Super Star Destroyer.

FIX-IT MAN HAN SOLO!

55

STAR WARS THE EMPIRE STRIKES BACK

STORY

FIX-IT MAN HAN SOLO™!

Navigating his ship through a belt of threatening asteroids, Solo readies his trump card: the jump to lightspeed. But at the crucial moment his equipment fails! Instantly, the pirate-turned-Rebel captain begins some emergency repairs...

DIGEST

COMING NEXT...
A Sudden Change of Plan

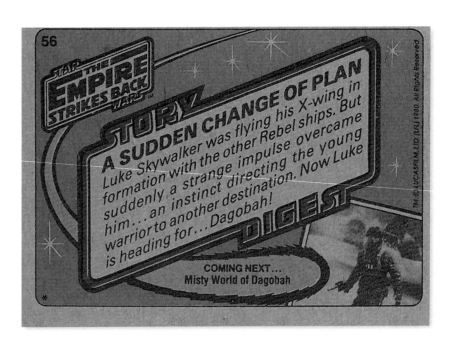

56

STAR THE EMPIRE WARS STRIKES BACK™

STORY DIGEST

A SUDDEN CHANGE OF PLAN

Luke Skywalker was flying his X-wing in formation with the other Rebel ships. But suddenly a strange impulse overcame him... an instinct directing the young warrior to another destination. Now Luke is heading for... Dagobah!

COMING NEXT...
Misty World of Dagobah

A SUDDEN CHANGE OF PLAN

Luke's impulse to leave Hoth for Dagobah and seek out the great Jedi Master Yoda is finally covered here.

MISTY WORLD OF DAGOBAH

57

THE EMPIRE STRIKES BACK

STORY

MISTY WORLD OF DAGOBAH™

Was it a dream, a hallucination, or simply the will of Ben Kenobi that led young Luke Skywalker to this mysterious planet of Dagobah in search of a Jedi Master named Yoda?

DIGEST

COMING NEXT...
The Creature Called Yoda

THE CREATURE CALLED YODA

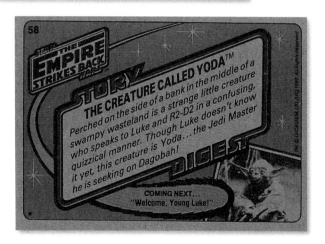

EMPIRE
STRIKES BACK

STORY

THE CREATURE CALLED YODA™

Perched on the side of a bank in the middle of a swampy wasteland is a strange little creature who speaks to Luke and R2-D2 in a confusing, quizzical manner. Though Luke doesn't know it yet, this creature is Yoda...the Jedi Master he is seeking on Dagobah!

DIGEST

COMING NEXT...
"Welcome, Young Luke!"

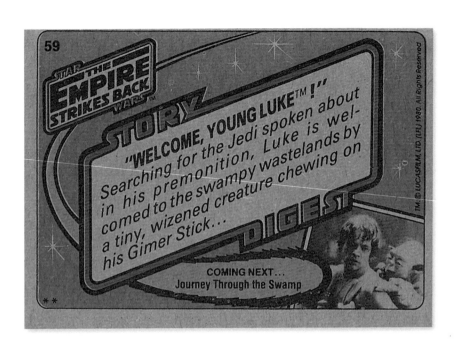

59

STAR WARS THE EMPIRE STRIKES BACK™

STORY

"WELCOME, YOUNG LUKE™!"

Searching for the Jedi spoken about in his premonition, Luke is welcomed to the swampy wastelands by a tiny, wizened creature chewing on his Gimer Stick...

DIGEST

COMING NEXT...
Journey Through the Swamp

"WELCOME, YOUNG LUKE!"

This card offers a dialogue caption that I simply made up and Lucasfilm
approved. Although the somewhat low-key nature of the line doesn't jive
with Yoda's initially eccentric behavior and speaking style (which at the time I
had not yet heard), it seemed to fit the moment nicely.

JOURNEY THROUGH THE SWAMP

60

STORY

JOURNEY THROUGH THE SWAMP

As a quizzical R2-D2 looks on, the tiny creature known as Yoda jumps on Luke's back and enjoys a free ride to the little being's home in the swamps of Dagobah...

COMING NEXT...
Yoda's House

DIGEST

The card description here is incorrect. As fans of the film know, a bewildered Luke follows Yoda to his little home on foot. The piggyback business occurs sometime later, during Luke's subsequent Jedi training.

YODA'S HOUSE

61

THE EMPIRE STRIKES BACK™

STORY

YODA'S™ HOUSE

The quaint abode belonging to Yoda is very much like its tenant: small, unassuming, but dignified and with a peculiar charm that fascinates young Luke.

COMING NEXT...
Artoo Peeking Through

ARTOO PEEKING THROUGH

62

ARTOO™ PEEKING THROUGH

Artoo-Deeto, curious about Luke's new friendship with the odd little creature from Dagobah, lifts his mechanical legs to their limit and peeks into the house where Luke and Yoda are dining...

COMING NEXT...
The Secret of Yoda

THE SECRET OF YODA

63

STAR WARS THE EMPIRE STRIKES BACK

STORY

THE SECRET OF YODA™

Yoda finally admits that he is the Jedi Master Luke was sent to uncover. Like his father before him, and like Ben Kenobi, Luke will now become apprentice to Yoda and learn with moral precision the ways of the Force!

DIGEST

COMING NEXT...
The Princess Lends A Hand

THE PRINCESS LENDS A HAND

64

STORY

THE PRINCESS LENDS A HAND

Having outrun the Imperial Star Destroyers, Han drives his vessel into a gaping cavern on one of the asteroids. Now, with hyperdrive capabilities still in grave doubt, Princess Leia joins in the repairing process.

DIGEST

COMING NEXT...
Repairing Hyperdrive

TM. © LUCASFILM LTD (LFL) 1980. All Rights Reserved.

REPAIRING HYPERDRIVE

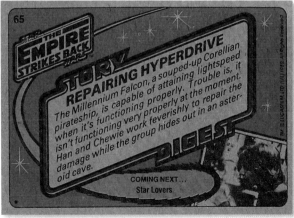

65

THE EMPIRE STRIKES BACK

STORY

REPAIRING HYPERDRIVE

The Millennium Falcon, a souped-up Corellian pirateship, is capable of attaining lightspeed when it's functioning properly. Trouble is, it isn't functioning very properly at the moment. Han and Chewie work feverishly to repair the damage while the group hides out in an asteroid cave.

DIGEST

COMING NEXT...
Star Lovers

STAR LOVERS

66

THE EMPIRE STRIKES BACK

STORY

STAR LOVERS

Take one devil-may-care space pirate, add a willful but sensitive princess too long burdened by her duty, and love—the oldest, truest force in this universe or any other—takes control for the moment.

COMING NEXT...
"Pardon Me Sir, But...Ohhh!"

A moment so memorable it required two cards. Han and Leia take their romantic relationship to a new level . . .

"PARDON ME SIR, BUT . . . OHHH!"

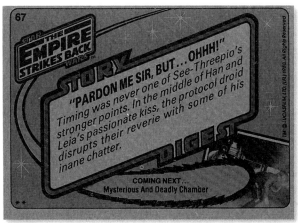

67

EMPIRE
STAR THE ... STRIKES BACK WARS

STORY

"PARDON ME SIR, BUT... OHHH!"
Timing was never one of See-Threepio's
stronger points. In the middle of Han and
Leia's passionate kiss, the protocol droid
disrupts their reverie with some of his
inane chatter.

DIGEST

COMING NEXT...
Mysterious And Deadly Chamber

. . . only to be interrupted by an annoyingly helpful C-3PO, who updates the "star lovers" on the *Falcon's* repairs. Another made-up dialogue caption from yours truly. Putting words into C-3PO's metallic mouth was a great deal of fun.

MYSTERIOUS AND DEADLY CHAMBER

68

THE EMPIRE STRIKES BACK

STORY

MYSTERIOUS AND DEADLY CHAMBER

Han, Leia and Chewie don gas masks while exploring the weird—and strangely moist—cavern they are hiding in while the Falcon is being repaired.

COMING NEXT...
Attacked by Batlike Creatures!

ATTACKED BY BATLIKE CREATURES!

69

STAR THE EMPIRE STRIKES BACK WARS

STORY

ATTACKED BY BATLIKE CREATURES!

Mynocks are five-feet-long tan, batlike creatures that fly in packs and are fond of attaching themselves to the hulls of available spacecraft...a habit that doesn't sit too well with pilot Han Solo!

COMING NEXT...
"Use the Force, Luke!"

A cool shot of Han blasting a mynock. At least we were able to show one of the cable-chewing beasties.

70

STAR THE EMPIRE STRIKES BACK WARS™

STORY

"USE THE FORCE, LUKE™!"

Back on Dagobah, Yoda's Jedi instructions have begun. Luke, using mental, physical and moral power, begins to master the ways of the Force as his unrelenting tutor observes his actions...

DIGEST

COMING NEXT...
Raising Luke's X-Wing

"USE THE FORCE, LUKE!"

RAISING LUKE'S X-WING

71

THE EMPIRE STRIKES BACK

STORY

RAISING LUKE'S X-wing™

With incredible psychic powers acquired with a mastery of the Force, Yoda raises the sunken X-wing Fighter from the bowels of the Dagobah swamp...

DIGEST

COMING NEXT...
A Need Beyond Reason

No cave test is mentioned in the card text, just megapowerful Yoda using the Force to raise Luke's downed X-wing fighter.

A NEED BEYOND REASON

An apprehensive Yoda conveys his concern that Luke might succumb to the dark side, like former pupil Darth Vader, although the direct connection between young Skywalker and his black-clad Sith enemy is glossed over.

A GATHERING OF EVILS

73

STAR WARS THE EMPIRE STRIKES BACK™

STORY

A GATHERING OF EVILS

Place: the Executor, Darth Vader's ominous space vessel. Present: a hand-picked collection of some of the meanest, most notorious bounty hunters in the Universe, brought together by the Dark Lord for a very special contest...

DIGEST

COMING NEXT...
The Bounty Hunters

I always liked this caption, a play on the title of the movie *A Gathering of Eagles*. The bounty hunters assembled by Darth Vader were so unique and colorful they warranted a three-card treatment.

THE BOUNTY HUNTERS

74

STAR THE EMPIRE STRIKES BACK WARS

STORY

THE BOUNTY HUNTERS

Among the evil participants assembled by Lord Vader: Dengar and Zuckuss, two unsavory, human type bounty hunters, and the tentacled Bossk, an amphibious monster whose soft baggy face houses two huge bloodshot eyes.

COMING NEXT...
IG-88 and Boba Fett

75

THE EMPIRE STRIKES BACK

STORY

IG-88 AND BOBA FETT™

Bounty hunter droid IG-88 and the notorious, mysterious Boba Fett join in Darth Vader's plan to capture Han Solo and his Rebel friends.

DIGEST

COMING NEXT...
Enter Lando Calrissian

IG-88 AND BOBA FETT

ENTER LANDO CALRISSIAN

76

STAR THE EMPIRE STRIKES BACK WARS

STORY

ENTER LANDO CALRISSIAN™

The gaseous planet of Bespin, located within the Bespin system, is the home of Cloud City. Here, intergalactic rogue Lando Calrissian has made a sizeable fortune as administrator of the thriving establishment.

DIGEST

COMING NEXT...
Warm Welcome for an Old Buddy

TM & © LUCASFILM LTD. (LFL) 1980 All Rights Reserved

WARM WELCOME FOR AN OLD BUDDY

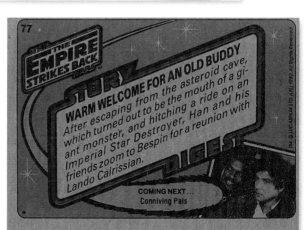

77

EMPIRE STRIKES BACK

WARM WELCOME FOR AN OLD BUDDY

After escaping from the asteroid cave, which turned out to be the mouth of a giant monster, and hitching a ride on an Imperial Star Destroyer, Han and his friends zoom to Bespin for a reunion with Lando Calrissian.

COMING NEXT...
Conniving Pals

Here is another wonderful photograph that captures the engaging personalities of key *Empire* characters: Bold but wary Han Solo has clearly met his smooth-talking match in old friend Lando Calrissian, who has apparently become a semirespectable businessman.

CONNIVING PALS

78

EMPIRE
STRIKES BACK

STORY

CONNIVING PALS

Han needs Lando's help to repair the light-speed capabilities of the Falcon. No sooner does Solo arrive on the Bespin scene than the two old buddies resume the friendly rivalry that has seen them through numerous adventures in the past...

DIGEST

COMING NEXT...
"Greetings, Sweet Lady"

"GREETINGS, SWEET LADY"

79

STAR WARS—THE EMPIRE STRIKES BACK™

STORY

"GREETINGS, SWEET LADY"

As a distantly jealous Han Solo looks on, Lando extends an enthusiastic welcome to Princess Leia. The princess, however, is a bit suspicious of the smooth-talking space rogue, and resolves to keep an eye on him...

DIGEST

COMING NEXT...
Calrissian's Main Man

Another made-up dialogue caption that suits the image quite well, conveying both Lando's silky-smooth charm and Leia's guarded skepticism.

CALRISSIAN'S MAIN MAN

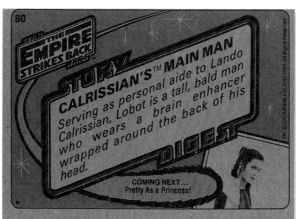

80

STAR WARS THE EMPIRE STRIKES BACK

STORY

CALRISSIAN'S™ MAIN MAN

Serving as personal aide to Lando Calrissian, Lobot is a tall, bald man who wears a brain enhancer wrapped around the back of his head.

DIGEST

COMING NEXT...
Pretty As a Princess!

Lando's aide, Lobot (John Hollis), gets a little attention in this nicely lit close-up.

PRETTY AS A PRINCESS!

81

THE EMPIRE STRIKES BACK

STORY

PRETTY AS A PRINCESS!
Han is all tongue-tied as Princess Leia, having changed into an exquisite evening dress, appears softer and more lovely than ever before.

DIGEST

COMING NEXT...
A Swarm of Ugnaughts

Many fans were surprised that Princess Leia's distinctive hairstyle from the first movie was changed for *Empire*. Interestingly, the follow-up film's storyboards still depicted Leia with the double-doughnut 'do because that was the only hairstyle that artists knew about at the time.

A SWARM OF UGNAUGHTS

82

THE EMPIRE STRIKES BACK

STORY

A SWARM OF UGNAUGHTS™
Chewie makes an important discovery while observing the Ugnaughts ... weird, piglike creatures that dwell in Cloud City and act both as scavengers and all-purpose henchmen.

DIGEST

COMING NEXT...
Threepio ... Blasted to Bits!

THREEPIO . . . BLASTED TO BITS!

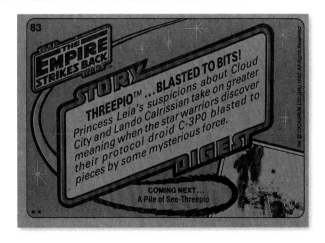

83

STORY

THREEPIO™ . . . BLASTED TO BITS!

Princess Leia's suspicions about Cloud City and Lando Calrissian take on greater meaning when the star warriors discover their protocol droid C-3PO blasted to pieces by some mysterious force.

DIGEST

COMING NEXT...
A Pile of See-Threepio

TM. © LUCASFILM LTD. (LFL) 1980 All Rights Reserved.

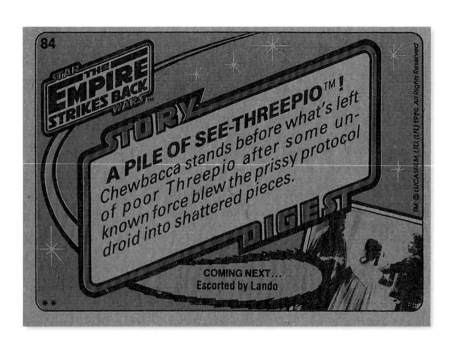

84

STAR WARS THE EMPIRE STRIKES BACK

STORY

A PILE OF SEE-THREEPIO™!
Chewbacca stands before what's left of poor Threepio after some un- known force blew the prissy protocol droid into shattered pieces.

DIGEST

COMING NEXT...
Escorted by Lando

A PILE OF SEE-THREEPIO!

ESCORTED BY LANDO

85

STAR THE EMPIRE STRIKES BACK WARS

STORY DIGEST

ESCORTED BY LANDO™

Han still can't believe his old pal, Lando Calrissian, might be up to no good, as Princess Leia suspects. Fears aside for the moment, the group is escorted to a Cloud City dining room...

COMING NEXT...
Dinner Guests

DINNER GUESTS

86

TM: © LUCASFILM LTD (DFL) 1980. All Rights Reserved

THE **EMPIRE** STRIKES BACK™

STORY DIGEST

DINNER GUESTS

Han, Chewie and Leia are led into the Cloud City dining chamber by Lando Calrissian. What they find there isn't on the menu…!

COMING NEXT…
Host of Horror

**

87

STAR WARS
THE EMPIRE STRIKES BACK™

STORY DIGEST

HOST OF HORROR

At the head of the dining chamber table is a vision of devastating horror. Lord Darth Vader, the Dark Lord, the harbinger of hate, now stands before the Rebel heroes he has sought so desperately since the Death Star raid.

COMING NEXT...
Deflecting Solo's Blasts

**

HOST OF HORROR

DEFLECTING SOLO'S BLASTS

88

STAR WARS THE **EMPIRE STRIKES BACK** TM

STORY

DEFLECTING SOLO'S™ BLASTS

Instinctively, Han Solo whips out his blaster and fires at the menacing figure of Darth Vader. But with a sweep of his hand, the Dark Lord easily deflects the oncoming peril and calls to his guards for assistance...

DIGEST

COMING NEXT...
Alas, Poor Threepio!

ALAS, POOR THREEPIO!

I couldn't resist this obvious caption, which everyone at Lucasfilm got a kick out of.

THE ORDEAL

90

EMPIRE STRIKES BACK

STORY

THE ORDEAL
Captured by Darth Vader and the bounty hunter Boba Fett, Han Solo undergoes a gruelling torture as his friends, locked in their cells, wait pensively...

DIGEST

COMING NEXT...
The Prize of Boba Fett

TM © LUCASFILM LTD (LFL) 1980 All Rights Reserved

THE PRIZE OF BOBA FETT

An iconic image of Darth Vader and his bounty hunter confederate, Boba Fett, with an increasingly concerned Lando Calrissian behind them.

92

STORY

HIS DAY OF TRIUMPH

This will be a day long remembered by the Empire, Vader thinks to himself. It has seen the capture of Han Solo and Princess Leia, and may soon see the end of the Rebellion itself!

DIGEST

COMING NEXT...
The Carbon-freezing Chamber

HIS DAY OF TRIUMPH

Canny *Star Wars* fans will recognize the rhythms of my back copy, which repeat Vader's grandiose proclamations to Grand Moff Tarkin from the first movie, with some slight adjustments to the current situation.

THE CARBON-FREEZING CHAMBER

93

THE EMPIRE STRIKES BACK

STORY

THE CARBON-FREEZING CHAMBER

All seems lost as Princess Leia, Han Solo and Chewbacca are led to an ominous, smoke-filled chamber by their villainous captors.

COMING NEXT...
End of the Star Warriors?

END OF THE STAR WARRIORS?

94

STAR THE **EMPIRE** STRIKES BACK

STORY

END OF THE STAR WARRIORS?

In this mysterious and nightmarish chamber, what devilish plans can Darth Vader have in store for the captured star heroes? Lando Calrissian is wondering also, since Vader tricked the Cloud City administrator into delivering his friends by promising that they wouldn't be harmed.

DIGEST

COMING NEXT...
Pawn of the Evil One

PAWN OF THE EVIL ONE

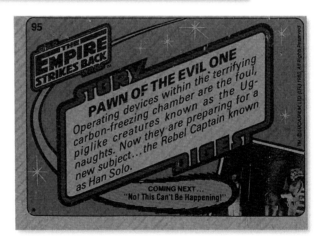

Nice close-up of an Ugnaught about to carbon-freeze Han Solo. The "evil one" of our card caption refers to Darth Vader.

"NO! THIS CAN'T BE HAPPENING!"

96

STORY

"NO! THIS CAN'T BE HAPPENING!" cries Prin-
"I've always loved you, Han" cess Leia. "I guess I never wanted to ad-
mit that—even to myself." The princess,
stunned with horror, watches through
tear-filled eyes as the gallant Han Solo is
led to his doom...

COMING NEXT...
The Fate of Han Solo

There is a lot of made-up dialogue in this card, all of it spoken by a
heartbroken Princess Leia. The caption itself was meant to convey what
the movie audience might be feeling at this moment, as Solo faces an
excruciating fate of living death. His earnest "I know" response to Leia's
proclamation of love was a famous Harrison Ford ad-lib, and therefore not in
any screenplay we were using for reference.

THE FATE OF HAN SOLO

97

STORY

THE FATE OF HAN SOLO™

As Han Solo's body becomes immersed in liquid flame, a suddenly relieved Lando observes that his friend has not been killed; rather, Han's bodily functions have merely been suspended by the carbon-freezing process for an indefinite period...

DIGEST

COMING NEXT...
Boba's Special Delivery

BOBA'S SPECIAL DELIVERY

98

STAR WARS THE EMPIRE STRIKES BACK

STORY

BOBA'S™ SPECIAL DELIVERY

His task essentially completed, the mysterious bounty hunter Boba Fett has the suspended body of Han Solo carried to his spaceship for a quick delivery to Jabba the Hut.

DIGEST

COMING NEXT...
Observed by Luke

OBSERVED BY LUKE

99

STAR WARS THE EMPIRE STRIKES BACK

STORY

OBSERVED BY LUKE™
Luke Skywalker finally arrives in Cloud City...just in time to see bounty hunter Boba Fett march off with the carbon-frozen body of his pal Han!

DIGEST

COMING NEXT...
Luke Arrives

LUKE ARRIVES

100

STORY

LUKE™ ARRIVES

With a determination bordering on fixation, Luke makes his way through the Cloud City corridors in search of his nemesis, the evil Darth Vader.

DIGEST

COMING NEXT...
Ready for Action!

READY FOR ACTION!

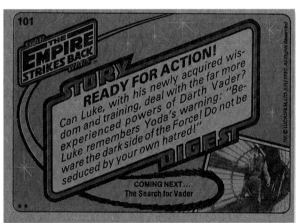

101

STAR THE EMPIRE STRIKES BACK WARS

STORY

READY FOR ACTION!

Can Luke, with his newly acquired wisdom and training, deal with the far more experienced powers of Darth Vader? Luke remembers Yoda's warning: "Beware the dark side of the Force! Do not be seduced by your own hatred!"

DIGEST

COMING NEXT...
The Search for Vader

THE SEARCH FOR VADER

102

THE EMPIRE STRIKES BACK

STORY

THE SEARCH FOR VADER™

In the cool, antiseptic corridors of Cloud City, Young Luke continues his search for the villainous Dark Lord of the Sith, Darth Vader.

DIGEST

COMING NEXT...
"Where Are You, Skywalker?"

"WHERE ARE YOU, SKYWALKER?"

103

STORY

"WHERE ARE YOU, SKYWALKER™?"

Darth Vader: the hunted... or the hunter? "Skywalker is a great threat to the Empire, a great threat to me," Vader thinks to himself. "If my trap succeeds, his own powers will be turned against him!"

COMING NEXT...
Dark Lord of the Sith

There is a good deal of made-up dialogue for this card, too, with its full view of the carbon-freeze chamber and nefarious Vader skulking about. The Dark Lord's scheme to turn Luke's own powers against him vaguely connects to the truth: In *Return of the Jedi*, Vader and the Emperor use young Skywalker's great faith in his father's potential for redemption to lure Luke into captivity.

DARK LORD OF THE SITH

104

STAR WARS
THE EMPIRE STRIKES BACK

STORY

DARK LORD OF THE SITH
He is the personification of evil, the dark, ruthless, power-hungry despot whose iron fist has shattered many a planet. He is...Lord Darth Vader.

DIGEST

COMING NEXT...
Weapon of Light

105

STAR WARS THE EMPIRE STRIKES BACK

STORY DIGEST

WEAPON OF LIGHT

The lightsaber, an elegant weapon used in the old days by the Jedi Knights, glows brightly in the hand of Darth Vader during his relentless search for young Luke.

COMING NEXT...
The Confrontation

WEAPON OF LIGHT

THE CONFRONTATION

106

STORY

THE CONFRONTATION

The moment is now at hand. Luke Skywalker, young former farmer from Tatooine, and Darth Vader, right hand man to the powerful Emperor, utilize the powers of the Force for a spectacular duel to the death...

DIGEST

COMING NEXT...
Duel of the Lightsabers

DUEL OF THE LIGHTSABERS

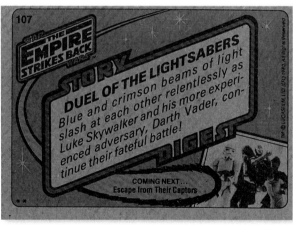

107

STORY

DUEL OF THE LIGHTSABERS

Blue and crimson beams of light slash at each other relentlessly as Luke Skywalker and his more experienced adversary, Darth Vader, continue their fateful battle!

DIGEST

COMING NEXT...
Escape from Their Captors

ESCAPE FROM THEIR CAPTORS

108

EMPIRE STRIKES BACK

STORY

ESCAPE FROM THEIR CAPTORS

As Luke and Vader wage their battle, Princess Leia, Chewie and Threepio (now strapped to the Wookiee's back) manage to escape from the stormtroopers with the aid of a guilt-ridden Lando Calrissian.

COMING NEXT...
Lando... Friend or Foe?

LANDO . . FRIEND OR FOE?

109

STORY

LANDO™ . . . FRIEND OR FOE?
Knowing only that Calrissian was
responsible for the fate of Han Solo,
Chewie turns his Wookiee's rage on
Lando. "Call him off, Princess!" gasps
the rattled space rogue. "I'm on your side
now!"

COMING NEXT...
Leia Takes Control!

My made-up dialogue was a lot more to the point than what director Irvin Kershner derived from Lando's strangulation dilemma. But this semicomedic moment added much to the scene, along with C-3PO's unhelpful explanation to gasping-for-breath Lando (". . . he's only a Wookiee!").

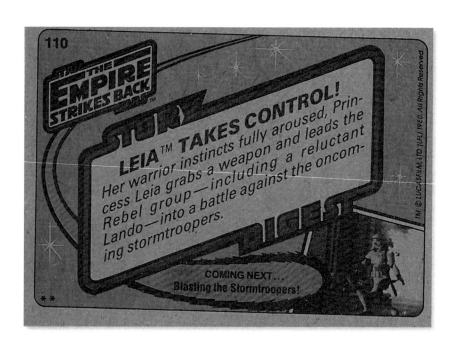

110

STAR THE **EMPIRE** STRIKES BACK

STORY

LEIA™ TAKES CONTROL!

Her warrior instincts fully aroused, Princess Leia grabs a weapon and leads the Rebel group—including a reluctant Lando—into a battle against the oncoming stormtroopers.

COMING NEXT...
Blasting the Stormtroopers!

**

LEIA TAKES CONTROL!

BLASTING THE STORMTROOPERS!

111

EMPIRE
STRIKES BACK

BLASTING THE STORMTROOPERS™!
The Cloud City corridors echo with
laserfire as Leia, Lando, Chewie and
Threepio pit their warrior skills
against the Imperial stormtroopers!

COMING NEXT...
Artoo to the Rescue!

ARTOO TO THE RESCUE!

112

STAR THE EMPIRE STRIKES BACK WARS

ARTOO™ TO THE RESCUE!
After what seems like an eternity, R2-D2 is reunited with his friends as the group fights their way through the ever-present dangers of Cloud City.

COMING NEXT...
Spectacular Battle!

SPECTACULAR BATTLE!

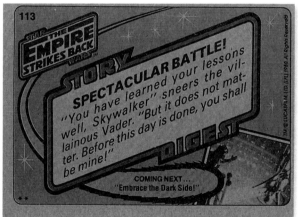

113

STAR THE EMPIRE STRIKES BACK WARS

STORY

SPECTACULAR BATTLE!
"You have learned your lessons well, Skywalker," sneers the villainous Vader. "But it does not matter. Before this day is done, you shall be mine!"

DIGEST

COMING NEXT...
"Embrace the Dark Side!"

TM. © LUCASFILM. LTD. (LFL) 1980. All Rights Reserved.

Once again I provided some made-up dialogue that fit the situation.

"EMBRACE THE DARK SIDE!"

114

STAR WARS THE EMPIRE STRIKES BACK

STORY DIGEST

"EMBRACE THE DARK SIDE!"

Luke, fighting with incredible skill, tries to cloud his mind from Vader's unyielding psychological attack. "I mustn't succumb to the dark side of the Force," Luke reminds himself again and again...

COMING NEXT...
"Hate Me, Luke! Destroy Me!"

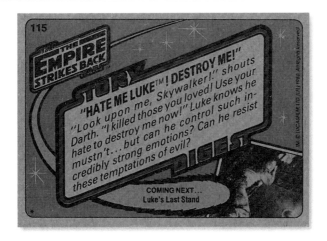

"HATE ME, LUKE! DESTROY ME!"

This made-up dialogue captures the essence of dark side temptation, exhorting the full embrace of hatred and rage. It would soon be echoed by Emperor Palpatine in *Return of the Jedi*.

LUKE'S LAST STAND

116

STAR WARS THE EMPIRE STRIKES BACK

STORY

LUKE'S™ LAST STAND

With the Cloud City in chaos, Luke holds on for dear life as Lord Vader disappears from view. Finally, the young star warrior is rescued by a familiar spaceship... the Millennium Falcon, now piloted by Princess Leia!

DIGEST

COMING NEXT...
"Do You Have a Foot In My Size?"

"DO YOU HAVE A FOOT IN MY SIZE?"

117

STORY

"DO YOU HAVE A FOOT IN MY SIZE?"

The adventure is ended...but only for now. A reflective Luke questions the measure of his success against Vader, while Leia, heartbroken, wonders what will become of Han Solo. Only the droids seem reasonably trouble free, for their internal injuries can be easily repaired. Ours, quite frequently...cannot.

DIGEST

STARTING NEXT CARD . . .
Exciting Space Paintings and Movie Facts

Wow. We certainly tied up the *Empire* story line quickly, with both Luke's off-screen rescue and the team's postescape plans to go after carbon-frozen Han Solo spoken about in broad terms. There's no mention of how R2-D2 interrupts C-3PO's foot repair to whisk the *Millennium Falcon* to safety with a hyperspace push. But based on prior experience, Topps realized that a second series of cards was inevitable, and additional opportunities to cover key events more fully would present themselves.

The remaining cards in our original *Empire* series are featured in a subset
called "Space Paintings," a collection of production illustrations rendered by
Star Wars designer extraordinaire Ralph McQuarrie. Instead of discussing this
specific artwork on the backs, we resurrected the Star Facts motif from our
1977 and 1978 sets to offer behind-the-scenes comments in general, starting
with a brief overview of creator George Lucas. Data about the actors, special
effects, and new characters are included over the course of thirteen cards.

SPACE PAINTINGS
by RALPH McQUARRIE

FALCON ON HOTH

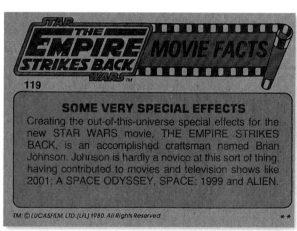

MOVIE FACTS

119

SOME VERY SPECIAL EFFECTS

Creating the out-of-this-universe special effects for the new STAR WARS movie, THE EMPIRE STRIKES BACK, is an accomplished craftsman named Brian Johnson. Johnson is hardly a novice at this sort of thing, having contributed to movies and television shows like 2001: A SPACE ODYSSEY, SPACE: 1999 and ALIEN.

SPACE PAINTINGS
by RALPH McQUARRIE

SNOW WALKERS™

MOVIE FACTS

120

THE SOUND OF THE STARS

STAR WARS was a breakthrough movie for many reasons, musical scoring among them. Composer John Williams almost single-handedly brought back symphonic music to the movies. His work includes JAWS, THE TOWERING INFERNO, SUPERMAN, DRACULA, STAR WARS and now, THE EMPIRE STRIKES BACK.

* *

SPACE PAINTINGS
by RALPH McQUARRIE

THE PURSUED

EMPIRE STRIKES BACK MOVIE FACTS

121

FROM LUCAS TO LUKE

When George Lucas first penned STAR WARS, his main character, Luke Skywalker, captured the author's own sense of awe and adventure. Through Luke, Lucas could fly great spaceships, fight dastardly villains, and save the entire universe. Through the sensitive performance of Mark Hamill, Luke's adventures come to life for millions of imaginative youngsters.

* *

SPACE PAINTINGS
by RALPH McQUARRIE

DARTH VADER™

MOVIE FACTS

122

CARRY ON, CARRIE!

Cute and perky Carrie Fisher, who re-creates the role of Princess Leia in THE EMPIRE STRIKES BACK, was born into the world of show business. Carrie has great affection for her Princess Leia role, and is pleased that the character will be more fully developed in EMPIRE.

* *

SPACE PAINTINGS
by RALPH McQUARRIE

SWAMPS OF DAGOBAH™

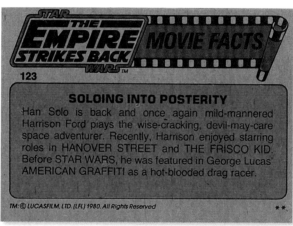

THE EMPIRE STRIKES BACK

MOVIE FACTS

123

SOLOING INTO POSTERITY

Han Solo is back and once again mild-mannered Harrison Ford plays the wise-cracking, devil-may-care space adventurer. Recently, Harrison enjoyed starring roles in HANOVER STREET and THE FRISCO KID. Before STAR WARS, he was featured in George Lucas' AMERICAN GRAFFITI as a hot-blooded drag racer.

**

SPACE PAINTINGS
by RALPH McQUARRIE

CLOUD CITY

124

A BRAND NEW STAR

Well . . . not really. Billy Dee Williams has been making movies and television shows for a long time. But he is new to the regular cast of characters in THE EMPIRE STRIKES BACK. Billy Dee plays Lando Calrissian, an old pal of Han's who has given up a pirate's life to be administrator of Bespin's Cloud City. He gets his friends in — and out — of jams during the course of the movie.

* *

SPACE PAINTINGS
by RALPH McQUARRIE

LANDO'S GREETING

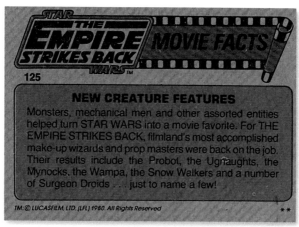

125

NEW CREATURE FEATURES

Monsters, mechanical men and other assorted entities helped turn STAR WARS into a movie favorite. For THE EMPIRE STRIKES BACK, filmland's most accomplished make-up wizards and prop masters were back on the job. Their results include the Probot, the Ugnaughts, the Mynocks, the Wampa, the Snow Walkers and a number of Surgeon Droids . . . just to name a few!

* *

SPACE PAINTINGS
by RALPH McQUARRIE

THREEPIO'S DESTRUCTION

126

SCENE-STEALING YODA™

Who is Yoda? He's quite possibly the greatest new star in the STAR WARS sequel, THE EMPIRE STRIKES BACK. Although just a few feet tall, Yoda, 800-year-old Jedi master and the fellow who taught Obi-Wan Kenobi everything he knows, has a winning personality that might just upstage his nuts-and-bolts rival Artoo in the charm sweepstakes!

* *

SPACE PAINTINGS
by RALPH McQUARRIE

LUKE BATTLING DARTH

STAR
THE
EMPIRE
STRIKES BACK
WARS ™

MOVIE FACTS

127

SPACECRAFT: THIS YEAR'S MODELS

Back from STAR WARS are the Millennium Falcon, X-wing and TIE Fighters and Imperial Star Destroyers. But new spaceships appearing in THE EMPIRE STRIKES BACK include the Executor, Darth Vader's ominous vessel, and Boba Fett's ship Slave I.

★ ★

SPACE PAINTINGS
by RALPH McQUARRIE

THE FINAL STAND

MOVIE FACTS

128

THE TRUTH ABOUT DARTH™

Darth Vader in STAR WARS: He was once a Jedi Knight,
one of Obi-Wan Kenobi's students before being seduced
by the dark side of the Force. Severely injured in battle, he
is outfitted in life-supporting armor from head to toe. In
THE EMPIRE STRIKES BACK, you may catch a glimpse
of what the Dark Lord truly looks like.

＊＊

SPACE PAINTINGS
by RALPH McQUARRIE

RESCUE

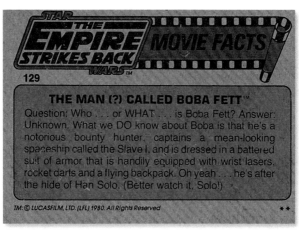

MOVIE FACTS

129

THE MAN (?) CALLED BOBA FETT

Question: Who . . . or WHAT . . . is Boba Fett? Answer: Unknown. What we DO know about Boba is that he's a notorious bounty hunter, captains a mean-looking spaceship called the Slave I, and is dressed in a battered suit of armor that is handily equipped with wrist lasers, rocket darts and a flying backpack. Oh yeah . . . he's after the hide of Han Solo. (Better watch it, Solo!)

**

SPACE PAINTINGS
by RALPH McQUARRIE

ION CANNON

THE EMPIRE STRIKES BACK

MOVIE FACTS

130

THEIR NEXT ADVENTURE

Amidst thunderous applause THE EMPIRE STRIKES BACK concludes, with Luke and Leia staring into a heavenly tapestry of stars and planets. Where do they go from here? Is Han Solo really doomed? Will Lando prove himself a true friend when the chips are down? Can Threepio learn to control his chattering? These and other questions will indeed be answered . . . next time around. BE THERE!

**

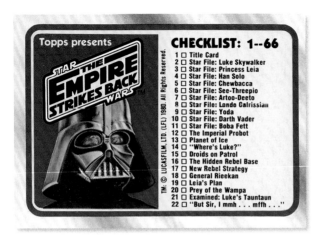

Topps presents

STAR THE EMPIRE STRIKES BACK WARS ™

CHECKLIST: 1--66

1 □ Title Card
2 □ Star File: Luke Skywalker
3 □ Star File: Princess Leia
4 □ Star File: Han Solo
5 □ Star File: Chewbacca
6 □ Star File: See-Threepio
7 □ Star File: Artoo-Deeto
8 □ Star File: Lando Calrissian
9 □ Star File: Yoda
10 □ Star File: Darth Vader
11 □ Star File: Boba Fett
12 □ The Imperial Probot
13 □ Planet of Ice
14 □ "Where's Luke?"
15 □ Droids on Patrol
16 □ The Hidden Rebel Base
17 □ New Rebel Strategy
18 □ General Rieekan
19 □ Leia's Plan
20 □ Prey of the Wampa
21 □ Examined: Luke's Tauntaun
22 □ "But Sir, I mmh . . . mffh . . ."

131 CHECKLIST continues

23 □ In Search of Luke
24 □ Frozen Death
25 □ Skywalker's Rescue
26 □ Luke's Fight for Life
27 □ Rejuvenation Chamber
28 □ Surgeon Droid
29 □ Artoo's Icy Vigil
30 □ Metal Monster
31 □ Zeroing In On Chewie!
32 □ Han Aims for Action!
33 □ Destroying the Probot
34 □ Death of Admiral Ozzel
35 □ The Freedom Fighters
36 □ Rebel Defenses
37 □ Armed Against the Enemy
38 □ Joined by Dack
39 □ The Sound of Terror
40 □ Suddenly . . . Starfire!
41 □ Rattled by the Enemy
42 □ Might of the Imperial Forces
43 □ The Snow Walkers
44 □ Luke . . . Trapped!

45 □ Escape from Icy Peril
46 □ "Retreat! Retreat!"
47 □ Headquarters in Shambles
48 □ Solo's Makeshift Escape
49 □ Invaded!
50 □ Vader and the Snowtroopers
51 □ Snowtroopers of the Empire
52 □ Millennium Falcon: Getaway Ship!
53 □ Emergency Blast Off!
54 □ Battle of the Star Destroyer
55 □ Fix-it Man Han Solo!
56 □ A Sudden Change of Plan
57 □ Misty World of Dagobah
58 □ The Creature Called Yoda
59 □ "Welcome, Young Luke!"
60 □ Journey Through the Swamp
61 □ Yoda's House
62 □ Artoo Peeking Through
63 □ The Secret of Yoda
64 □ The Princess Lends A Hand
65 □ Repairing Hyperdrive
66 □ Star Lovers

NOTE: Piece together the EMPIRE STRIKES BACK puzzle with the backs of the stickers!

Not surprisingly, two Checklist cards were needed to contain all the necessary data for this expanded trading card set.

Topps presents

CHECKLIST: 67-132

67 □ "Pardon Me Sir, But . . . Ohhh!"
68 □ Mysterious And Deadly Chamber
69 □ Attacked by Batlike Creatures!
70 □ "Use the Force, Luke!"
71 □ Raising Luke's X-Wing
72 □ A Need Beyond Reason
73 □ A Gathering of Evils
74 □ The Bounty Hunters
75 □ IG-88 and Boba Fett
76 □ Enter Lando Calrissian
77 □ Warm Welcome for an Old Buddy
78 □ Conniving Pals
79 □ "Greetings, Sweet Lady"
80 □ Calrissian's Main Man
81 □ Pretty As a Princess!
82 □ A Swarm of Ugnaughts
83 □ Threepio . . . Blasted to Bits!
84 □ A Pile of See-Threepio
85 □ Escorted by Lando
86 □ Dinner Guests
87 □ Host of Horror
88 □ Deflecting Solo's Blasts

---

132   CHECKLIST continues

89 □ Alas, Poor Threepio!
90 □ The Ordeal
91 □ The Prize of Boba Fett
92 □ Nis Day of Triumph
93 □ The Carbon-freezing Chamber
94 □ End of the Star Warriors?
95 □ Pawn of the Evil One
96 □ "No! This Can't Be Happening!"
97 □ The Fate of Han Solo
98 □ Boba's Special Delivery
99 □ Observed by Luke
100 □ Luke Arrives
101 □ Ready for Action!
102 □ The Search for Vader
103 □ "Where Are You, Skywalker?"
104 □ Dark Lord of the Sith
105 □ Weapon of Light
106 □ The Confrontation
107 □ Duel of the Lightsabers
108 □ Escape from Their Captors
109 □ Lando . . . Friend or Foe?
110 □ Leia Takes Control!

111 □ Blasting the Stormtroopers!
112 □ Artoo to the Rescue!
113 □ Spectacular Battle!
114 □ "Embrace the Dark Side!"
115 □ "Hate Me, Luke! Destroy Me!"
116 □ Luke's Last Stand
117 □ "Do You Have a Foot In My Size?"
118 □ Paintings: Probot
119 □ Paintings: Falcon On Hoth
120 □ Paintings: Snow Walkers
121 □ Paintings: The Pursued
122 □ Paintings: Darth Vader
123 □ Paintings: Swamps of Dagobah
124 □ Paintings: Cloud City
125 □ Paintings: Lando's Greeting
126 □ Paintings: Threepio's Destruction
127 □ Paintings: Luke Battling Darth
128 □ Paintings: The Final Stand
129 □ Paintings: Rescue
130 □ Paintings: Ion Cannon
131 □ Checklist: 1--66
132 □ Checklist: 67-132

NOTE: Piece together the EMPIRE STRIKES BACK puzzle
with the backs of the stickers!

There were thirty-three stickers in this set; the first twenty-two were letter shaped. All these years later, it's unclear why the full alphabet was not represented.

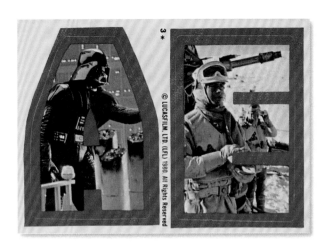

3 *

4 **

5 **

6 *

7 **

8 *

9 **

10 *

13 **

14 **

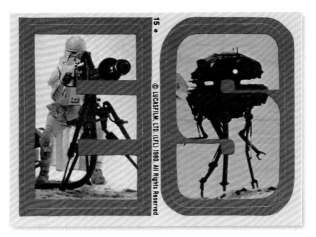

17 **

18 *

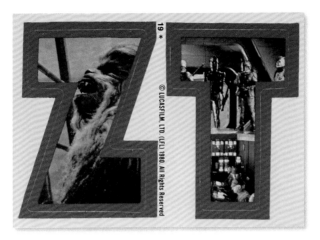

19 *

20 *

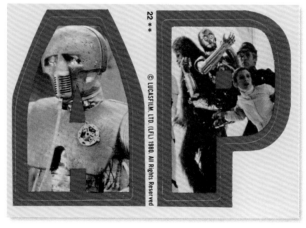

23
*

24
**

25
**

* 26

* 27

28
* *

29
*

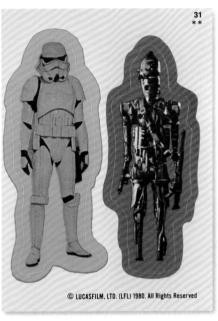

32
**

33
**

HERE IS WHAT YOUR COMPLETED
RED BORDER PUZZLE WILL LOOK LIKE:

COLLECT ALL 15 CARDS OF PUZZLE A.

Ready for action: This dramatic shot of our heroes was chosen to be the Series 1 puzzle.

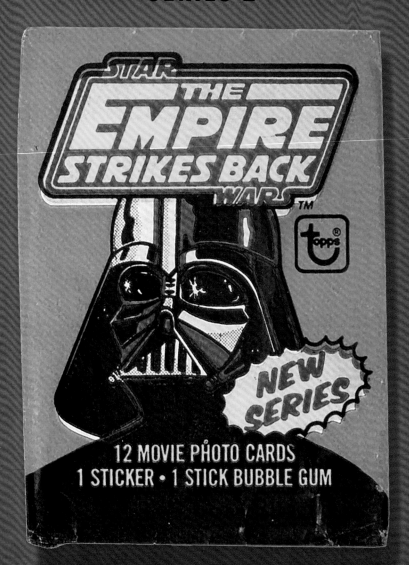

The Empire Strikes Back provided a movie poster painting that blew everyone away, a kind of *Gone with the Wind* vista that emphasized Leia and Han's romance. This key art didn't arrive in time for Topps to use it in Series 1, but it became the breathtaking title card of our second set. It is also employed as the puzzle for the sticker backs of Series 2.

STARCRAFT

MILLENNIUM FALCON

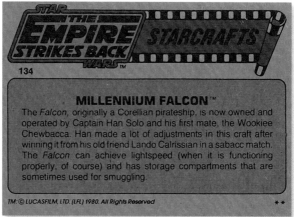

134

MILLENNIUM FALCON™

The *Falcon*, originally a Corellian pirateship, is now owned and operated by Captain Han Solo and his first mate, the Wookiee Chewbacca. Han made a lot of adjustments in this craft after winning it from his old friend Lando Calrissian in a sabacc match. The *Falcon* can achieve lightspeed (when it is functioning properly, of course) and has storage compartments that are sometimes used for smuggling.

* *

One of the subsets that elevated the quality of Series 2 was a group we called "Starcraft," which essentially takes the place of a character-card lineup. These spaceships are so imaginative and distinctive that they are practically characters in their own right. Each of the studio models was shot against a black screen, and Topps's art department added the star field background later.

STARCRAFT

THE EXECUTOR

135

THE EXECUTOR™

The largest and most fearsome of the Imperial Star Destroyers, the *Executor* is Darth Vader's spaceship. Its topside resembles a metropolitan skyline in size and shape, and its long, narrow form lends a properly ominous look to this, the Dark Lord's personal space vehicle.

* *

STARCRAFT

IMPERIAL STAR DESTROYER

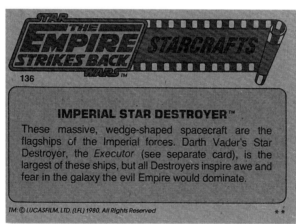

136

IMPERIAL STAR DESTROYER™

These massive, wedge-shaped spacecraft are the flagships of the Imperial forces. Darth Vader's Star Destroyer, the *Executor* (see separate card), is the largest of these ships, but all Destroyers inspire awe and fear in the galaxy the evil Empire would dominate.

**

STARCRAFT

TWIN-POD CLOUD CAR

STARCRAFTS

137

TWIN-POD CLOUD CAR™

Cloud cars are the main form of transportation on Bespin's Cloud City. These graceful flying vehicles are composed of two cubiclelike pods connected by an engine structure that powers the craft. They escorted the *Millennium Falcon* safely into the city and into the unpredictable hands of Lando Calrissian.

* *

STARCRAFT

SLAVE I

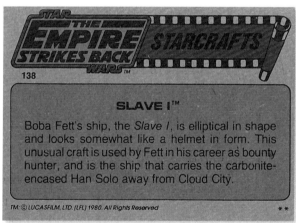

138

SLAVE I™

Boba Fett's ship, the *Slave I*, is elliptical in shape and looks somewhat like a helmet in form. This unusual craft is used by Fett in his career as bounty hunter, and is the ship that carries the carbonite-encased Han Solo away from Cloud City.

TM: © LUCASFILM, LTD. (LFL) 1980. All Rights Reserved **

REBEL ARMORED SNOWSPEEDER

139

REBEL ARMORED SNOWSPEEDER™

These highly maneuverable, two-man vehicles are flown by the Rebels on the ice planet Hoth. Small, snub-nosed craft, the snowspeeders are especially useful in battling the slower, more awkward Imperial snow walkers which were dispatched by the Empire to obliterate the hidden Rebel base.

**

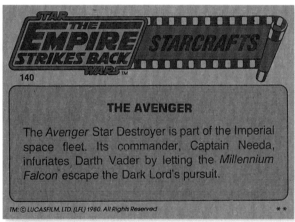

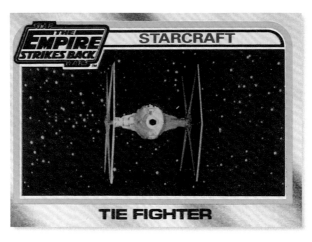

STARCRAFT

TIE FIGHTER

141

TIE FIGHTER™

The TIE fighter is a super-fast, highly efficient one-man fighting vehicle used extensively by the Imperial forces. These ships shoot twin lasers and are frequently pitted against the somewhat more graceful X-wing fighters of the Rebellion.

* *

STARCRAFT

REBEL TRANSPORT

142

REBEL TRANSPORT™

An extremely long, unusual-looking vehicle used by the Rebels for simple transportation or shuttling to other vehicles. This is not a combat ship, although its hull is constructed to ward off minor attacks from Imperial fighters.

* *

STARCRAFT

TIE BOMBER

STARCRAFTS

143

TIE BOMBER™

Essentially a variation or extension of the basic design of the TIE fighter, this spaceship is a threat from the Empire and has blasted many a Rebel fighter into stardust.

* *

PREPARING FOR BATTLE

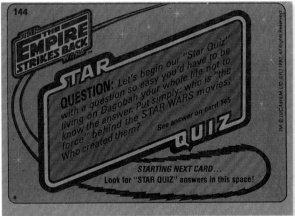

144

STAR

QUESTION: Let's begin our "Star Quiz" with a question so easy you'd have to be living on Dagobah your whole life not to know the answer. Put simply: who is "the force" behind the STAR WARS movies? Who created them?

See answer on card 145

STAR QUIZ

STARTING NEXT CARD...
Look for "STAR QUIZ" answers in this space!

Original subsets aside, the *Empire Strikes Back* story line was destined to be covered again in our second series, with different (or different enough) photos. Since repeating the plot on the backs seemed redundant, we introduced a new feature: Star Quiz, which asks questions that are answered at the bottom of the following card. Most are shockingly simple, such as this one.

SEEKING THE MISSING LUKE

TM © LUCASFILM LTD. (LFL) 1980. All Rights Reserved

145

STAR WARS THE EMPIRE STRIKES BACK

STAR

QUESTION: When and where do the STAR WARS adventures take place?

See answer on card 146

QUIZ

Answer to "STAR QUIZ" of card no. 144
George Lucas

THE SEARCHER

146

THE EMPIRE STRIKES BACK

STAR

QUESTION: What is Princess Leia's last name?

See answer on card 147

QUIZ

Answer to "STAR QUIZ" of card no. 145
A long time ago in a galazy far, far away

Here's a nice portrait shot of Luke Skywalker outside Echo Base.

STAR PILOT LUKE SKYWALKER

147

STAR WARS THE EMPIRE STRIKES BACK

STAR

QUESTION: What is the first spaceship ever to be seen in a STAR WARS movie? *See answer on card 148*

QUIZ

Answer to "STAR QUIZ" of card no. 146
Organa

** **

LUKE'S PATROL

148

STAR
THE EMPIRE STRIKES BACK
WARS

STAR

QUESTION: What does Princess Leia do and say to Luke just before they swing across the chasm in the Death Star?

See answer on card 149

QUIZ

Answer to "STAR QUIZ" of card no. 147
The Rebel Blockade Runner

TM © LUCASFILM LTD. (LFL) 1980. All Rights Reserved.

SHELTER ON ICY HOTH

149

THE EMPIRE STRIKES BACK

STAR

QUESTION: What is the name of the giant battle station des- troyed by Luke Skywalker in STAR WARS?

See answer on card 150

QUIZ

Answer to "STAR QUIZ" of card no. 148
She kisses him and says, "For luck"

IMPERIAL SPY

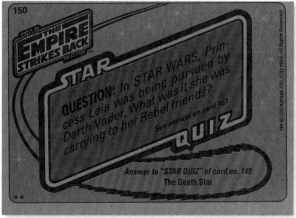

Deep focus and bold composition give this cool photo its power as the distant Imperial probot prepares a sneak attack on Han Solo.

TRACKING THE PROBOT

151

THE **EMPIRE** STRIKES BACK™

STAR

QUESTION: In STAR WARS, what was the name of the spaceship Princess Leia was escaping in at the beginning of the story?

See answer on card 152

QUIZ

Answer to "STAR QUIZ" of card no. 150
Intercepted information about the Death Star

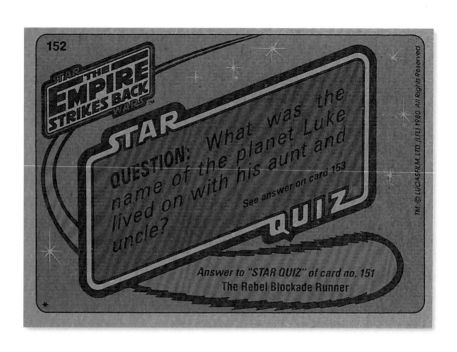

152

THE EMPIRE STRIKES BACK

STAR

QUESTION: What was the name of the planet Luke lived on with his aunt and uncle?

See answer on card 153

QUIZ

Answer to "STAR QUIZ" of card no. 151
The Rebel Blockade Runner

HAN SOLO, RESCUER

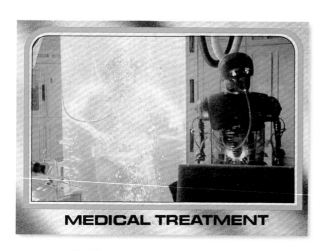

MEDICAL TREATMENT

153

STAR WARS THE EMPIRE STRIKES BACK™

STAR

QUESTION: How many years has Yoda instructed young Jedi warriors?

See answer on card 154

QUIZ

Answer to "STAR QUIZ" of card no. 152
Tatooine

WORRIED DROIDS ON HOTH

154

STAR

QUIZ

QUESTION: Darth Vader is also known as the Dark Lord of the...?

See answer on card 155

Answer to "STAR QUIZ" of card no. 153
At least eight hundred years

IMPERIAL ASSAULT!

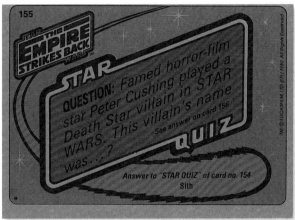

155

STAR

QUESTION: Famed horror-film star Peter Cushing played a Death Star villain in STAR WARS. This villain's name was...?

See answer on card 156

QUIZ

Answer to "STAR QUIZ" of card no. 154
Sith

When I first saw this and similar shots at Lucasfilm, I remember thinking how dark and realistic these "fighting in the trenches" scenes looked. I wondered if Lucas was making a sequel to *Star Wars* or to Stanley Kubrick's *Paths of Glory*.

NARROW ESCAPE!

TM © LUCASFILM LTD (LFL) 1980 All Rights Reserved

156

STAR

THE EMPIRE STRIKES BACK

QUESTION: In the beginning of STAR WARS, what sort of craft do Threepio and Artoo use to escape from the invaded Rebel Blockade Runner?

See answer on card 157

QUIZ

Answer to "STAR QUIZ" of card no. 155
Grand Moff Tarkin

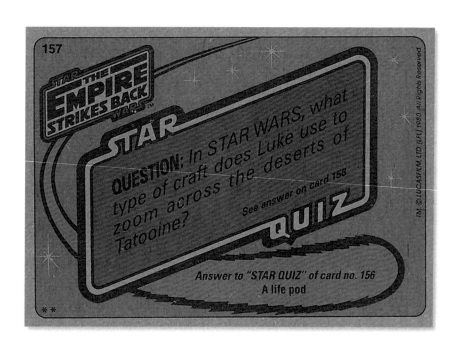

157

THE EMPIRE STRIKES BACK

STAR

QUESTION: In STAR WARS, what type of craft does Luke use to zoom across the deserts of Tatooine?

See answer on card 158

QUIZ

Answer to "STAR QUIZ" of card no. 156
A life pod

FIGHTING AGAINST THE EMPIRE

158

THE EMPIRE STRIKES BACK™

STAR

QUESTION: What was the name of Princess Leia's home planet?

See answer on card 159

QUIZ

Answer to "STAR QUIZ" of card no. 157
A landspeeder

**

ROAR OF THE WOOKIEE

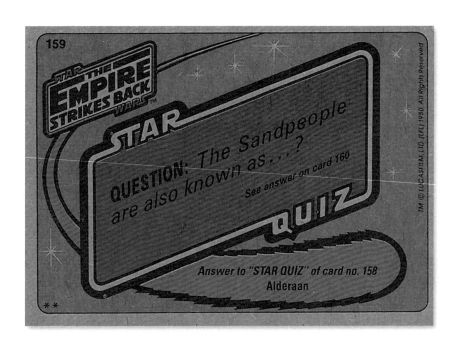

159

STAR WARS
THE EMPIRE STRIKES BACK™

STAR

QUESTION: The Sandpeople
are also known as . . . ?

See answer on card 160

QUIZ

Answer to "STAR QUIZ" of card no. 158
Alderaan

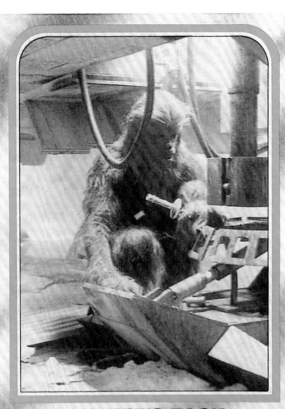

CHEWIE'S TASK

MOMENTS BEFORE THE ESCAPE

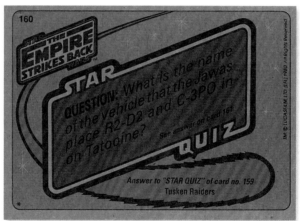

160

EMPIRE
STRIKES BACK

STAR

QUESTION: What is the name of the vehicle that the Jawas place R2-D2 and C-3PO in on Tatooine?

See answer on card 161

QUIZ

Answer to "STAR QUIZ" of card no. 159
Tusken Raiders

LAST STAGES OF THE BATTLE

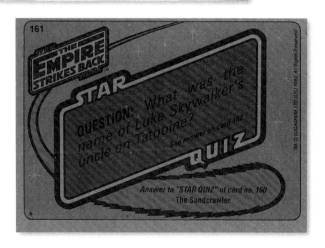

161

EMPIRE STRIKES BACK

STAR QUIZ

QUESTION: What was the name of Luke Skywalker's uncle on Tatooine?

See answer on card 162

Answer to "STAR QUIZ" of card no. 160
The Sandcrawler

162

THE EMPIRE STRIKES BACK

STAR

QUESTION: What was the name of Luke Skywalker's aunt on Tatooine?

See answer on card 163

QUIZ

Answer to "STAR QUIZ" of card no. 161
Owen Lars

GALLANT WARRIOR

"RAISE THOSE SHIPS!"

163

STAR THE EMPIRE STRIKES BACK™

STAR

QUESTION: Who was the master of Artoo and Threepio before Luke Skywalker?

See answer on card 164

QUIZ

Answer to "STAR QUIZ" of card no. 162
Beru

THE AWESOME ONE

164

STAR WARS THE EMPIRE STRIKES BACK™

STAR

QUESTION: The Sandpeople travel across the sandy wastes of Tatooine on the backs of huge, furry creatures. These beasts are known as . . . ?

See answer on card 165

QUIZ

Answer to "STAR QUIZ" of card no. 163
Captain Antilles

VADER AND HIS SNOWTROOPERS

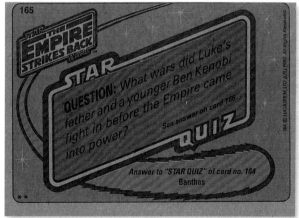

165

STAR

EMPIRE STRIKES BACK

QUESTION: What wars did Luke's father and a younger Ben Kenobi fight in before the Empire came into power?

See answer on card 166.

QUIZ

Answer to "STAR QUIZ" of card no. 164
Banthas

TAKEOVER OF REBEL BASE

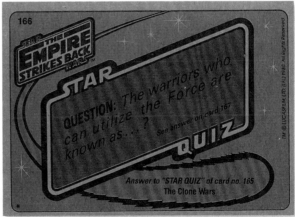

166

STAR THE EMPIRE STRIKES BACK

STAR

QUESTION: The warriors who can utilize the Force are known as...?

See answer on card 167

QUIZ

Answer to "STAR QUIZ" of card no. 165
The Clone Wars

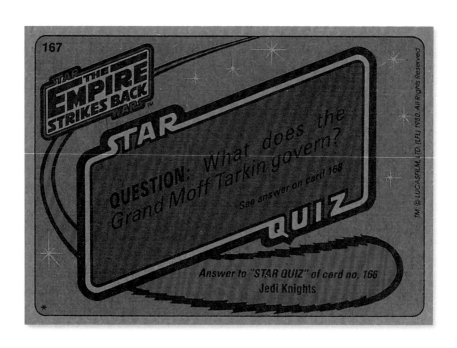

167

STAR WARS
THE EMPIRE STRIKES BACK™

STAR

QUESTION: What does the Grand Moff Tarkin govern?

*See answer on card 168

QUIZ

Answer to "STAR QUIZ" of card no. 166
Jedi Knights

THE MAN CALLED HAN SOLO

Nice full-figure portrait of Han Solo, the smuggler turned rebel destined to marry a plucky princess.

168

THE EMPIRE STRIKES BACK™

STAR

QUESTION: What government maintained order in the galaxy before the Empire came into being?

See answer on card 169

QUIZ

Answer to "STAR QUIZ" of card no. 167
Imperial outland regions

**

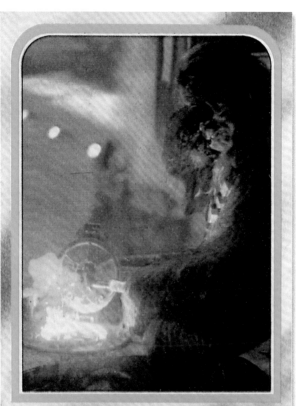

THE FALCON IN REPAIRS

169

THE EMPIRE STRIKES BACK ™

STAR

QUESTION: How do Sandpeople ride to hide their numbers?

See answer on card 170

QUIZ

Answer to "STAR QUIZ" of card no. 168
The Old Republic

SKILLS OF THE STAR PILOT

170

THE EMPIRE STRIKES BACK

STAR

QUESTION: In STAR WARS, what was the name of the spaceport where Ben and Luke go looking for a pilot?

See answer on card 171

QUIZ

Answer to "STAR QUIZ" of card no. 169
Single file

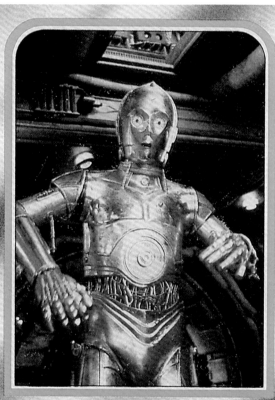

"SIR . . . WAIT FOR ME!"

HAN'S DESPERATE PLAN

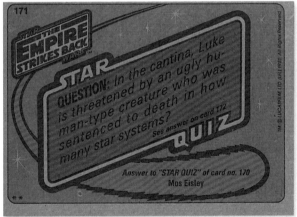

171

EMPIRE
STRIKES BACK

STAR

QUESTION: In the cantina, Luke is threatened by an ugly human-type creature who was sentenced to death in how many star systems?

See answer on card 172

QUIZ

Answer to "STAR QUIZ" of card no. 170
Mos Eisley

AN OVERWORKED WOOKIEE?

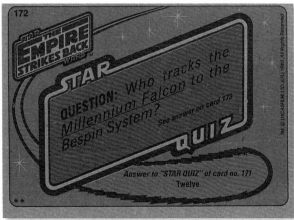

QUESTION: Who tracks the Millennium Falcon to the Bespin System?

See answer on card 173

Answer to "STAR QUIZ" of card no. 171
Twelve

"OH, HELLO THERE, CHEWBACCA!"

173

STAR

QUESTION: In the cantina, how much money does Han demand for his services before Ben suggests an alternative deal?

See answer on card 174

QUIZ

Answer to "STAR QUIZ" of card no. 172
The bounty hunter Boba Fett

More made-up dialogue for this caption, but it was in character for C-3PO. In the film, Chewbacca's head had an amusing tendency to pop out of unexpected places.

ARTOO'S BUMPY LANDING

174

STAR

THE EMPIRE STRIKES BACK

QUESTION: What is the number of the bay where the Millennium Falcon is docked at Mos Eisley spaceport?

See answer on card 175

QUIZ

Answer to "STAR QUIZ" of card no. 173
Ten thousand credits

MYSTERIOUS PLANET

175

STAR WARS THE EMPIRE STRIKES BACK

STAR

QUESTION: What is the name of the green-skinned alien who tries to subdue Han Solo in the cantina?

See answer on card 176

QUIZ

Answer to "STAR QUIZ" of card no. 174
Docking Bay 94

"LUKE. . .IN TROUBLE?"

176

THE EMPIRE STRIKES BACK

STAR

QUESTION: Who put a price on Han Solo's head?

See answer on card 177

QUIZ

Answer to "STAR QUIZ" of card no. 175
Greedo

WORKING AGAINST TIME

177

EMPIRE STRIKES BACK

STAR

QUESTION: What type of ship is the Millennium Falcon?

See answer on card 178

QUIZ

Answer to "STAR QUIZ" of card no. 176
Jabba the Hut

HAN AND THE PRINCESS

178

QUESTION: While addressing the bounty hunters, Darth Vader forbids what type of attack on our heroes?

See answer on card 179

QUIZ

Answer to "STAR QUIZ" of card no. 177
A Corellian pirateship

SOLDIERS OF THE EMPIRE

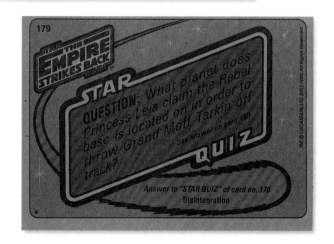

179

STAR

QUESTION: What planet does Princess Leia claim the Rebel base is located on in order to throw Grand Moff Tarkin off track?

See answer on card 180

QUIZ

Answer to "STAR QUIZ" of card no. 178
Disintegration

THE WOOKIEE AT WORK

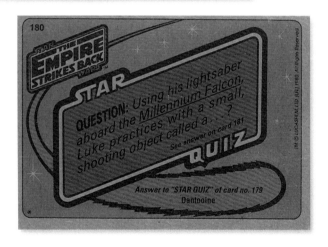

180

THE EMPIRE STRIKES BACK

STAR

QUESTION: Using his lightsaber aboard the Millennium Falcon, Luke practices with a small, shooting object called a . . ?

See answer on card 181

QUIZ

Answer to "STAR QUIZ" of card no. 179
Dantooine

VADER AND A BOUNTY HUNTER

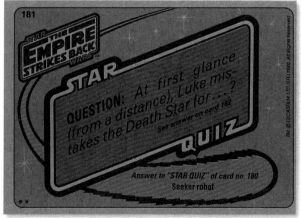

181

STAR

THE EMPIRE STRIKES BACK

QUESTION: At first glance (from a distance), Luke mistakes the Death Star for . . . ?

See answer on card 182

QUIZ

Answer to "STAR QUIZ" of card no. 180
Seeker robot

WORLD OF DARKNESS

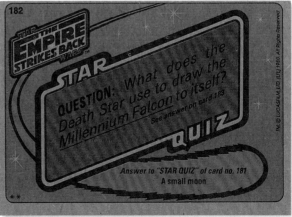

182

QUESTION: What does the Death Star use to draw the Millennium Falcon to itself?

See answer on card 183

Answer to "STAR QUIZ" of card no. 181
A small moon

Princess Leia's outfit seems to have changed color in this shot . . . or could it be that art director Ben Solomon and the Topps airbrushing department were being creative?

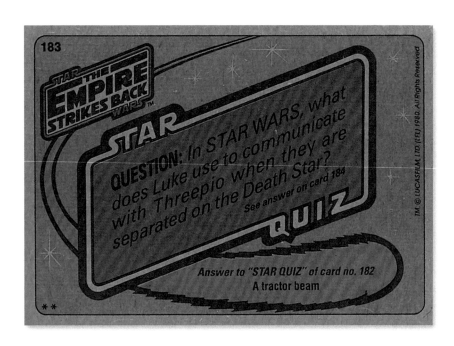

183

STAR WARS THE EMPIRE STRIKES BACK™

STAR

QUESTION: In STAR WARS, what does Luke use to communicate with Threepio when they are separated on the Death Star?

See answer on card 184

QUIZ

Answer to "STAR QUIZ" of card no. 182
A tractor beam

TAKING NO CHANCES!

FAREWELL TO YODA AND DAGOBAH

184

THE STAR WARS EMPIRE STRIKES BACK

STAR

QUESTION: What type of droid is See-Threepio?

See answer on card 185.

QUIZ

Answer to "STAR QUIZ" of card no. 183
A comlink

An evocative image of Luke having a meaningful exchange with Yoda just before blasting off for Cloud City. An optically inserted Obi-Wan would join them in the finished film.

RACING TO THE FALCON

185

THE EMPIRE STRIKES BACK

STAR

QUESTION: What is Princess Leia's less-than-flattering nickname for Chewbacca in STAR WARS?

See answer on card 186

QUIZ

Answer to "STAR QUIZ" of card no. 184
A protocol droid

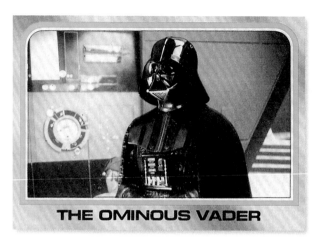

THE OMINOUS VADER

186

STAR WARS
THE EMPIRE STRIKES BACK

STAR

QUESTION: In STAR WARS, what device does Governor Tarkin use to track the Falcon after it escapes from the Death Star?

See answer on card 187

QUIZ

Answer to "STAR QUIZ" of card no. 185
A big walking carpet

THE DARK PURSUER

187

STAR QUIZ

QUESTION: In STAR WARS, the Rebel base is located on a moon orbiting what planet?

See answer on card 188

Answer to "STAR QUIZ" of card no. 186
A homing beacon

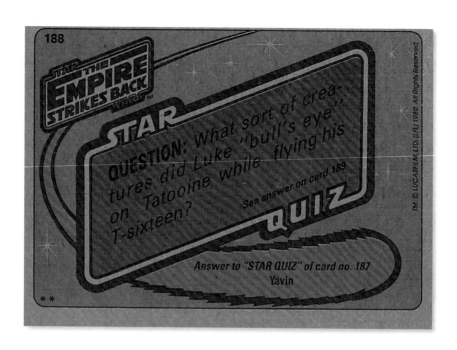

188

THE EMPIRE STRIKES BACK

STAR

QUESTION: What sort of creatures did Luke "bull's eye" on Tatooine while flying his T-sixteen?

See answer on card 189

QUIZ

Answer to "STAR QUIZ" of card no. 187
Yavin

**

YOUNG SENATOR FROM ALDERAAN

DON'T FOOL WITH HAN SOLO

189

STAR THE **EMPIRE STRIKES BACK** WARS™

STAR

QUESTION: What is Han Solo's reaction after he receives his medal from Princess Leia in the first film?

See answer on card 190

QUIZ

Answer to "STAR QUIZ" of card no. 188
Womp rats

TM. © LUCASFILM LTD (LFL) 1980. All Rights Reserved.

KINDRED SPIRITS

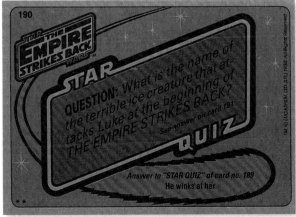

190

STAR

THE EMPIRE STRIKES BACK™

QUESTION: What is the name of the terrible ice creature that attacks Luke at the beginning of THE EMPIRE STRIKES BACK?

See answer on card 191

QUIZ

Answer to "STAR QUIZ" of card no. 189
He winks at her

**

LOBOT'S TASK

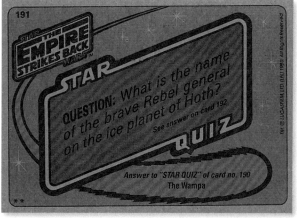

191

STAR THE EMPIRE STRIKES BACK WARS

STAR

QUESTION: What is the name of the brave Rebel general on the ice planet of Hoth?

See answer on card 192.

QUIZ

Answer to "STAR QUIZ" of card no. 190
The Wampa

A BRAVE PRINCESS

192

STAR THE EMPIRE STRIKES BACK WARS

STAR

QUIZ

QUESTION: What does Luke use to escape the deadly clutches of the ice creature on Hoth?

See answer on card 193

Answer to "STAR QUIZ" of card no. 191
General Rieekan

CORRIDORS OF BESPIN

193

STAR

QUESTION: What is the name of the surgeon droid who assists Luke in recovering from his injuries in EMPIRE?

See answer on card 194

QUIZ

Answer to "STAR QUIZ" of card no. 192
His lightsaber

TM. © LUCASFILM LTD. (LFL) 1980. All Rights Reserved.

LANDO'S AIDE, LOBOT

194

STAR

QUESTION: What color are Chewie's eyes?

See answer on card 195

QUIZ

Answer to "STAR QUIZ" of card no. 193
Too-Onebee (2-1B)

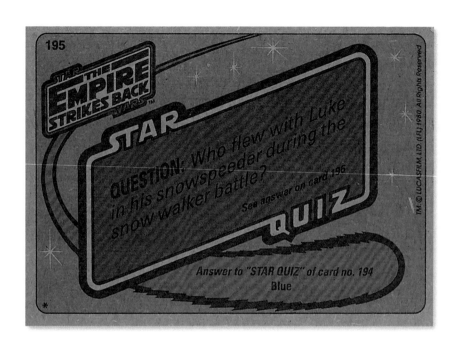

195

STAR WARS

THE EMPIRE STRIKES BACK™

STAR

QUESTION: Who flew with Luke in his snowspeeder during the snow walker battle?

See answer on card 196

QUIZ

Answer to "STAR QUIZ" of card no. 194
Blue

"GET BACK QUICK . . . IT'S VADER!"

Here's a dramatic image of Han speeding into action, on reflex and to no avail. Obviously he doesn't have time to speak my line of made-up dialogue in the actual movie, as Vader disarms him instantly.

HELD BY THE STORMTROOPERS

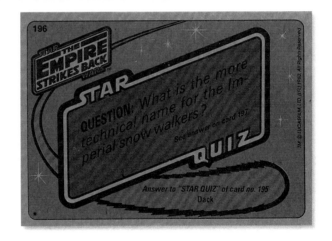

196

STAR
THE EMPIRE STRIKES BACK WARS™

STAR

QUESTION: What is the more technical name for the Imperial snow walkers?

See answer on card 197

QUIZ

Answer to "STAR QUIZ" of card no. 195
Dack

TM © LUCASFILM LTD. (LFL) 1982. All Rights Reserved

HAN'S TORMENT

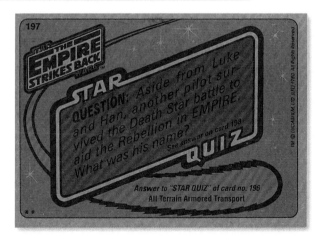

197

STAR WARS THE EMPIRE STRIKES BACK

STAR

QUESTION: Aside from Luke and Han, another pilot survived the Death Star battle to aid the Rebellion in EMPIRE. What was his name?

See answer on card 198

QUIZ

Answer to "STAR QUIZ" of card no. 196
All Terrain Armored Transport

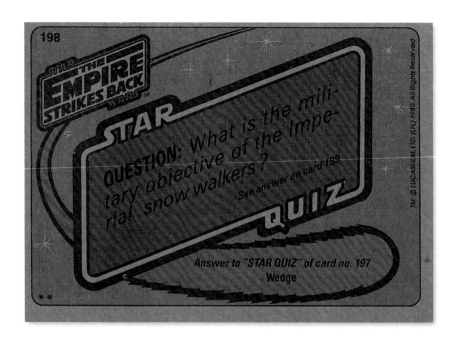

198

THE EMPIRE STRIKES BACK

STAR

QUESTION: What is the military objective of the Imperial snow walkers?

See answer on card 199

STAR QUIZ

Answer to "STAR QUIZ" of card no. 197
Wedge

LANDO'S GAME

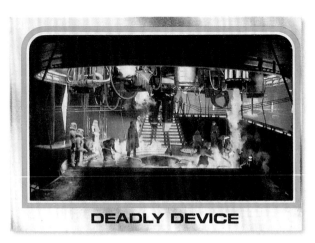

DEADLY DEVICE

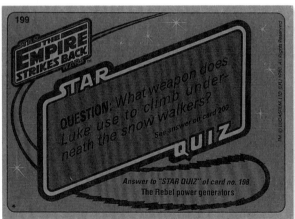

199

STAR WARS THE EMPIRE STRIKES BACK™

STAR

QUIZ

QUESTION: What weapon does Luke use to climb underneath the snow walkers?

See answer on card 200.

TM © LUCASFILM LTD (LFL) 1980. All Rights Reserved

Answer to "STAR QUIZ" of card no. 198
The Rebel power generators

IN VADER'S CLUTCHES

200

STAR

QUESTION: As the Millennium Falcon blasts out of the Rebel hangar on Hoth, the snowtroopers set up and attempt to use what type of weapon against our heroes?

See answer on card 201

QUIZ

Answer to "STAR QUIZ" of card no. 199
A harpoon gun

Nicely framed image of Leia on Bespin just before Han is frozen in carbonite. Lighting effects and compositions used in a film are often replicated by the on-set unit photographer, who in this case was George Whitear. Coverage of key scenes, most of it intended for publicity, is expected to capture the movie's visual personality as much as possible.

A TEARFUL FAREWELL

201

EMPIRE STRIKES BACK

STAR

QUESTION: After escaping from the ice creature on Hoth, Luke sees a mysterious vision of ...?

See answer on card 202

QUIZ

Answer to "STAR QUIZ" of card no. 200
A laser cannon

HAN FACES HIS FATE

202

QUESTION: What planet does the vision in the show tell Luke to journey to?

See answer on card 203

Answer to "STAR QUIZ" of card no. 201
Ben Kenobi

INTO THE CARBON-FREEZING PIT!

203

STAR

QUIZ

QUESTION: In EMPIRE, who is Luke told to seek out on the mysterious planet he is sent to?

See answer on card 204

Answer to "STAR QUIZ" of card no. 202
Dagobah

AN UGNAUGHT

204

THE EMPIRE STRIKES BACK

STAR QUIZ

QUESTION: To escape from the Star Destroyers after fleeing Hoth, Han sends the Millenium Falcon straight into a field of . . . ?

See answer on card 205.

Answer to "STAR QUIZ" of card no. 203
The Jedi Master, Yoda

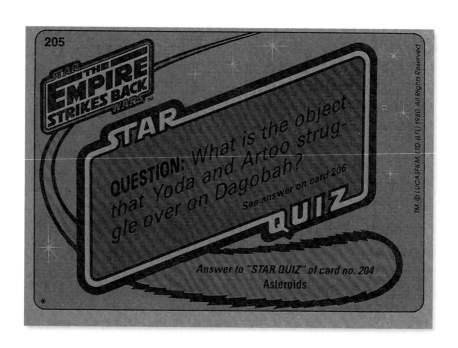

205

STAR WARS THE EMPIRE STRIKES BACK™

STAR

QUESTION: What is the object that Yoda and Artoo struggle over on Dagobah?

See answer on card 206

QUIZ

Answer to "STAR QUIZ" of card no. 204
Asteroids

TEARS OF A PRINCESS

SUSPENDED IN CARBON FREEZE

206

THE EMPIRE STRIKES BACK

STAR

QUESTION: What are the creatures that crawl around the hull of the Millennium Falcon inside the asteroid cave?

See answer on card 207

QUIZ

Answer to "STAR QUIZ" of card no. 205
A power lamp

GRUESOME FATE!

207

STAR

THE EMPIRE STRIKES BACK

QUESTION: What is Yoda a teacher of?

See answer on card 208

QUIZ

Answer to "STAR QUIZ" of card no. 206
Mynocks

EVIL THREATENS!

208

THE STAR WARS

EMPIRE STRIKES BACK

STAR

QUESTION: Using the Force,
Yoda raises what object from
the swamp of Dagobah?
See answer on card no. 209

QUIZ

Answer to "STAR QUIZ" of card no. 207
The ways of the Force

"THIS DEAL IS GETTING WORSE!"

209

STAR WARS THE EMPIRE STRIKES BACK™

STAR

QUESTION: In EMPIRE, what frequently needs to be re-paired on the Millennium Falcon?

See answer on card 210

QUIZ

Answer to "STAR QUIZ" of card no. 208
Luke's X-wing fighter

Here we have an actual line spoken by Lando Calrissian in the film, though this card attributes it to the wrong scene. But the sentiment is accurate, and the dialogue functions as a thought he might logically be having at this desperate juncture.

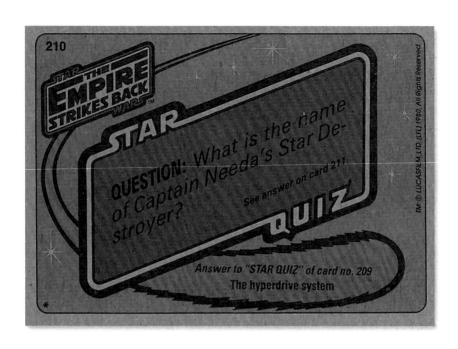

210

THE EMPIRE STRIKES BACK ™

STAR

QUESTION: What is the name of Captain Needa's Star Destroyer?

See answer on card 211

QUIZ

Answer to "STAR QUIZ" of card no. 209
The hyperdrive system

THE CAPTOR, BOBA FETT

FEAR ON CLOUD CITY

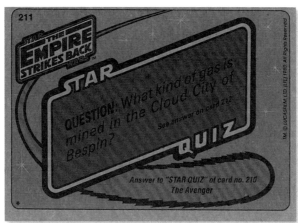

211

STAR THE EMPIRE STRIKES BACK STAR WARS™

STAR

QUESTION: What kind of gas is mined in the Cloud City of Bespin?

See answer on card 212

QUIZ

Answer to "STAR QUIZ" of card no. 210
The Avenger

A WARRIOR DRIVEN

212

THE EMPIRE STRIKES BACK

STAR

QUESTION: Name three bounty hunters assembled by Darth Vader (other than Boba Fett).

See answer on card 213

QUIZ

Answer to "STAR QUIZ" of card no. 211
Tibanna gas

COURAGE OF SKYWALKER

213

STAR WARS THE EMPIRE STRIKES BACK™

STAR QUIZ

QUESTION: What is the name of the three-pronged twig Yoda uses as a stick?

See answer on card 214

Answer to "STAR QUIZ" of card no. 212
Bossk, Dengar, IG-88, Zuckuss (any three)

THE PURSUER

214

THE EMPIRE STRIKES BACK

STAR

QUESTION: Who serves as personal aide to Lando Calrissian on Bespin?

See answer on card 215.

QUIZ

Answer to "STAR QUIZ" of card no. 213
Gimer Stick

215

THE EMPIRE STRIKES BACK™

STAR

QUESTION: Scavenging, pig-like creatures dwell in Cloud City. They are called...?

See answer on card 216

QUIZ

Answer to "STAR QUIZ" of card no. 214
Lobot

STALKED BY VADER!

A DROID GONE TO PIECES

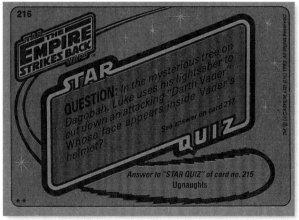

216

QUESTION: In the mysterious tree on Dagobah, Luke uses his lightsaber to cut down an attacking "Darth Vader." Whose face appears inside Vader's helmet?

See answer on card 217

Answer to "STAR QUIZ" of card no. 215
Ugnaughts

THREEPIO'S FREE RIDE

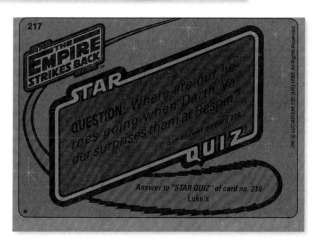

217

STAR WARS THE EMPIRE STRIKES BACK

STAR

QUESTION: Where are our heroes going when Darth Vader surprises them at Bespin?

See answer on card 218.

QUIZ

Answer to "STAR QUIZ" of card no. 216
Luke's

STORMTROOPER TAKEOVER!

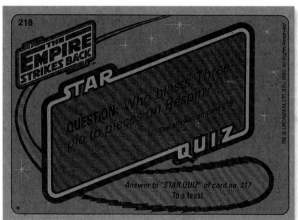

218

EMPIRE STRIKES BACK

STAR

QUESTION: Who blasts Threepio to pieces on Bespin?
See answer on card 219

QUIZ

Answer to "STAR QUIZ" of card no. 217
To a feast!

TM © LUCASFILM LTD. (LFL) 1980. All Rights Reserved

PRINCESS LEIA UNDER GUARD!

219

STAR · THE
EMPIRE
STRIKES BACK
WARS™

STAR

QUESTION: Who discovers the dismembered Threepio on Bespin?

See answer on card 220

QUIZ

Answer to "STAR QUIZ" of card no. 218
Stormtroopers

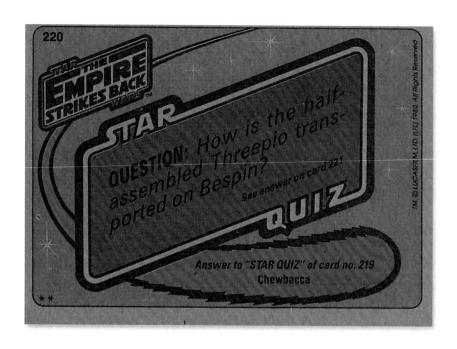

220

STAR WARS THE EMPIRE STRIKES BACK™

STAR

QUESTION: How is the half-assembled Threepio transported on Bespin?

See answer on card 221

QUIZ

Answer to "STAR QUIZ" of card no. 219
Chewbacca

**

BOUNTY HUNTER BOBA FETT

LANDO COVERS THEIR ESCAPE!

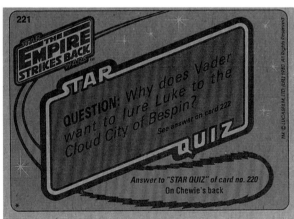

221

STAR

QUESTION: Why does Vader want to lure Luke to the Cloud City of Bespin?

See answer on card 222

QUIZ

Answer to "STAR QUIZ" of card no. 220
On Chewie's back

TUMBLING TO AN UNKNOWN FATE

222

STAR THE EMPIRE STRIKES BACK WARS™

STAR

QUESTION: In the carbon-freezing chamber Han is en-cased in what substance?

See answer on card 223

QUIZ™

Answer to "STAR QUIZ" of card no. 221
To seduce him to the dark side of the Force

223

STAR WARS
THE EMPIRE STRIKES BACK™

STAR

QUESTION: When Leia tells Han she loves him, what is his reply?

See answer on card 224

QUIZ

Answer to "STAR QUIZ" of card no. 222
Carbonite, a high quality alloy

ON THE VERGE OF DEFEAT!

Luke holds on for dear life after his dramatic free fall. This card pretty much ends the loose sequential approach employed for Series 2. The next group of pictures, still presented with Star Quiz as a back element, would be a potpourri of portraits, scenes, and posed setups.

224

STAR

QUESTION: In the climactic confrontation scene, what does Darth Vader implore Luke to use against him?

See answer on card 225

QUIZ

Answer to "STAR QUIZ" of card no. 223
"I know"

**

GIFTED PERFORMER

225

STAR WARS
THE EMPIRE STRIKES BACK

STAR

QUESTION: What terrible truth did Ben not reveal to Luke?

See answer on card 226

QUIZ

Answer to "STAR QUIZ" of card no. 224
Luke's hatred

ACTRESS CARRIE FISHER

226

STAR THE EMPIRE STRIKES BACK WARS™

STAR

QUESTION: What structure does Luke hold onto for dear life at the end of EMPIRE?

See answer on card 227

QUIZ

Answer to "STAR QUIZ" of card no. 225
Darth Vader is Luke's father

HAN SOLO (HARRISON FORD)

ANTHONY DANIELS AS C-3PO

227

EMPIRE
STRIKES BACK

STAR

QUESTION: Who first betrays
our heroes and later joins
them against Vader in
EMPIRE?

See answer on card 226

QUIZ

Answer to "STAR QUIZ" of card no. 226
An electronic weather vane

TM © LUCASFILM LTD (LFL) 1980 All Rights Reserved

* *

OUR FAVORITE PROTOCOL DROID

228

QUESTION: Who eventually fixes the hyperdrive system on the Millennium Falcon in the nick of time?

See answer on card 229

Answer to "STAR QUIZ" of card no. 227
Lando Calrissian

229

THE EMPIRE STRIKES BACK ™

STAR

QUESTION: What extremely important device does Luke receive at the very end of EMPIRE?

See answer on card 230

QUIZ

Answer to "STAR QUIZ" of card no. 228
R2-D2

**

R2-D2 (KENNY BAKER)

"MYNOCKS OUTSIDE? OH MY!"

230

QUESTION: Where is Luke heading at the very end of EMPIRE?

See answer on card 231

Answer to "STAR QUIZ" of card no. 229
A mechanical hand

ACTOR BILLY DEE WILLIAMS

231

STAR THE **EMPIRE** STRIKES BACK WARS

STAR

QUESTION: Where are Lando and Chewbacca heading at the very end of EMPIRE?

See answer on card 232

QUIZ

Answer to "STAR QUIZ" of card no. 230
Back to Tatooine

232

THE EMPIRE STRIKES BACK

QUESTION: What role did Anthony Daniels play in STAR WARS and THE EMPIRE STRIKES BACK?

See answer on card 233

TM © LUCASFILM LTD (LFL) 1980. All Rights Reserved

STAR QUIZ

Answer to "STAR QUIZ" of card no. 231
To rescue Han from Boba Fett

**

GALAXY'S MOST LOYAL DROIDS

This beautiful portrait of the droids on Hoth enjoyed an afterlife as one of Topps's oversized Photocards (page 543).

DASHING HAN SOLO

233

QUESTION: What role did Peter Mayhew play in STAR WARS and THE EMPIRE STRIKES BACK?

See answer on card 234

Answer to "STAR QUIZ" of card no. 232
See-Threepio

THE FORCE AND THE FURY

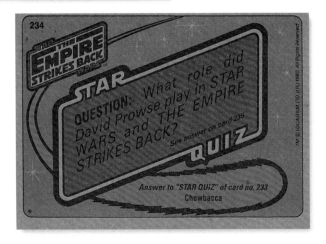

234

STAR

THE EMPIRE STRIKES BACK

QUESTION: What role did David Prowse play in STAR WARS and THE EMPIRE STRIKES BACK?

See answer on card 235.

QUIZ

Answer to "STAR QUIZ" of card no. 233
Chewbacca

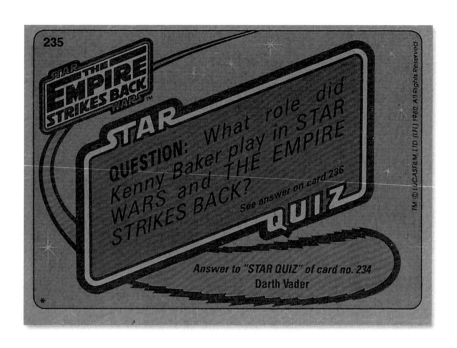

235

THE EMPIRE STRIKES BACK

STAR

QUESTION: What role did Kenny Baker play in STAR WARS and THE EMPIRE STRIKES BACK?

See answer on card 236

QUIZ

Answer to "STAR QUIZ" of card no. 234
Darth Vader

YODA'S SQUABBLE WITH R2-D2

BLASTED BY LEIA!

236

STAR WARS THE EMPIRE STRIKES BACK™

STAR

QUESTION: Who performs Yo-da in THE EMPIRE STRIKES BACK?

See answer on card 237

QUIZ

Answer to "STAR QUIZ" of card no. 235
Artoo-Detoo

TM © LUCASFILM LTD. (LFL) 1980. All Rights Reserved

THE ART OF LEVITATION

238

THE EMPIRE STRIKES BACK

STAR

QUESTION: Who composed the music for both STAR WARS FILMS?

See answer on card 239

STAR QUIZ

Answer to "STAR QUIZ" of card no. 237
James Earl Jones

SNOWSWEPT CHEWBACCA

DREAMWORLD . . . OR TRAP?

239

EMPIRE STRIKES BACK

STAR

QUESTION: Name the special-effects supervisors for THE EMPIRE STRIKES BACK.

See answer on card 240

QUIZ

Answer to "STAR QUIZ" of card no. 238
John Williams

SWAMPLAND PERIL!

240

THE EMPIRE STRIKES BACK™

STAR

QUESTION: What is the name of the special-effects organization that handled both STAR WARS films?

See answer on card 241

QUIZ

Answer to "STAR QUIZ" of card no. 239
Brian Johnson and Richard Edlund

Swamp world Dagobah undergoes a bizarre color change courtesy of an overcreative airbrushing from the Topps staff.

"TRIED, HAVE YOU?"

241

THE **EMPIRE** STRIKES BACK

STAR

QUESTION: Who is the produc-
er of STAR WARS and THE
EMPIRE STRIKES BACK?

See answer on card 242

QUIZ

Answer to "STAR QUIZ" of card no. 240
Industrial Light and Magic (ILM)

ENCOUNTER ON DAGOBAH

242

THE EMPIRE STRIKES BACK

STAR

QUESTION: George Lucas directed another movie that featured Harrison Ford (Han). What was it called?

See answer on card 243

QUIZ

Answer to "STAR QUIZ" of card no. 241
Gary Kurtz

CAPTAIN SOLO SENSES A TRAP

243

STAR THE EMPIRE STRIKES BACK WARS

STAR

QUESTION: Why is Han encased in carbonite?

See answer on card 244

QUIZ

Answer to "STAR QUIZ" of card no. 242
AMERICAN GRAFFITI

A TEST FOR LUKE

R2-D2 ON THE MISTY BOG

245

THE EMPIRE STRIKES BACK™
STAR WARS™

STAR

QUESTION: Will there be a sequel to THE EMPIRE STRIKES BACK?

See answer on card 246

QUIZ

Answer to "STAR QUIZ" of card no. 244
JAWS

CONFRONTING THE DARK SIDE

246

STAR WARS THE EMPIRE STRIKES BACK

STAR

QUESTION: How many films in the STAR WARS series are planned by George Lucas?

See answer on card 247

QUIZ

Answer to "STAR QUIZ" of card no. 245
Yes

247

THE EMPIRE STRIKES BACK

STAR

QUESTION: Alec Guinness, Ben Kenobi in both STAR WARS films, was honored at what American film event?

See answer on card 248

QUIZ

Answer to "STAR QUIZ" of card no. 246
A full nine

LUKE BATTLES . . . HIMSELF?

BLOOMING ROMANCE

248

QUESTION: What was the name of the science-fiction movie made by George Lucas before STAR WARS?

See answer on card 249

Answer to "STAR QUIZ" of card no. 247
The Academy Awards

CHEWIE RETALIATES

249

STAR

QUESTION: What character made his first appearance in the car-toon shown during THE STAR WARS HOLIDAY SPECIAL on TV in 1979?

See answer on card 260

QUIZ

Answer to "STAR QUIZ" of card no. 248
THX-1138

* *

STORMTROOPER BATTLE

250

QUESTION: How old is the Jedi Master Yoda?

See answer on card 251

Answer to "STAR QUIZ" of card no. 249
Boba Fett

I was always impressed by the airbrushing on this dramatic shot of Imperial troops downed by our heroes during their Cloud City escape.

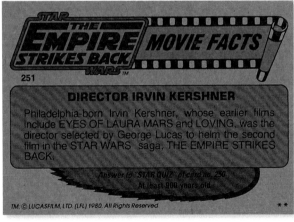

Just when the picture redundancy problem that plagued our original *Star Wars* sets began to surface again, along came this legitimately fresh behind-the-scenes subset, the closing act of Series 2. We dug our ever-popular Movie Facts moniker out of editorial mothballs to headline the various copy blocks on the backs.

SPIFFING UP A WOOKIEE™

For human beings, keeping one's hair in place can be a royal pain at times. But imagine being a Wookiee! During the filming of THE EMPIRE STRIKES BACK, it was the job of make-up artist Kay Freeborn to keep Chewbacca's body fur presentable and tangle-free for the cameras.

**

SPIFFING UP A WOOKIEE

FILMING THE FALCON

FILMING THE FALCON™

More than the ordinary motion picture, THE EMPIRE STRIKES BACK employed a dazzling array of full-sized props. Needless to say, most of the massive spaceships seen buzzing across the screen were miniature models constructed by the special effects crew. Sometimes, however, life-sized versions of the ships were needed when filming scenes with the human characters.

KERSHNER DIRECTS MARK HAMILL

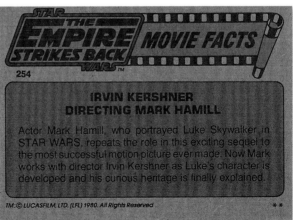

A great shot of director Irvin Kershner putting Mark Hamill through his paces for the Cloud City corridor sequence. Kershner brought his own creative integrity to this all-important assignment, allowing actors such as Harrison Ford to improvise freely.

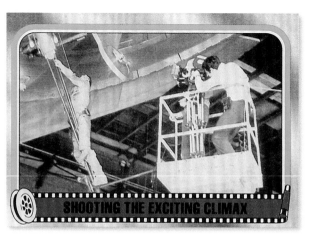

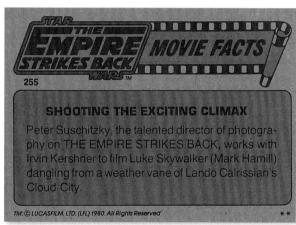

SHOOTING THE EXCITING CLIMAX

255

SHOOTING THE EXCITING CLIMAX

Peter Suschitzky, the talented director of photography on THE EMPIRE STRIKES BACK, works with Irvin Kershner to film Luke Skywalker (Mark Hamill) dangling from a weather vane of Lando Calrissian's Cloud City.

* *

FILMING VADER IN HIS CHAMBER

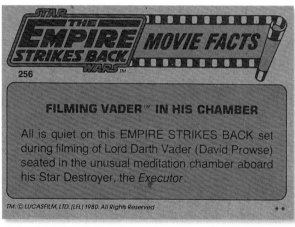

It is fascinating to see how Darth Vader was filmed in his personal meditation pod aboard the *Executor*.

DAGOBAH COMES TO LIFE

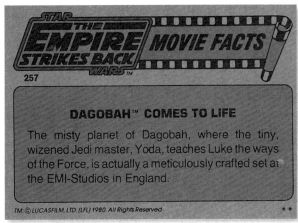

257

DAGOBAH™ COMES TO LIFE

The misty planet of Dagobah, where the tiny, wizened Jedi master, Yoda, teaches Luke the ways of the Force, is actually a meticulously crafted set at the EMI-Studios in England.

BUILDING THE FALCON

BUILDING THE FALCON™

The outer hull of the *Millennium Falcon* is readied for George Lucas' new space epic, THE EMPIRE STRIKES BACK. Once again this amazing Corellian pirateship is piloted by Han Solo (Harrison Ford) and his Wookiee co-pilot Chewbacca (Peter Mayhew).

* *

HOTH REBEL BASE SEQUENCE

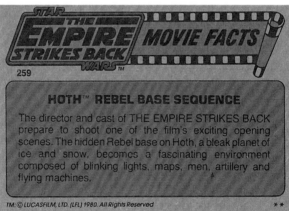

MOVIE FACTS

259

HOTH™ REBEL BASE SEQUENCE

The director and cast of THE EMPIRE STRIKES BACK prepare to shoot one of the film's exciting opening scenes. The hidden Rebel base on Hoth, a bleak planet of ice and snow, becomes a fascinating environment composed of blinking lights, maps, men, artillery and flying machines.

* *

FILMING AN EXPLOSION

MOVIE FACTS

260

FILMING AN EXPLOSION

Luke Skywalker, innocent farmer-turned-gallant warrior, battles the ominous Darth Vader in a chilling confrontation that reveals a most startling secret. This sequence required some unique set construction as well as carefully placed miniature explosions to be set off as the lightsabers slashed all objects in their paths.

SPECTACULAR SWAMPLAND SET

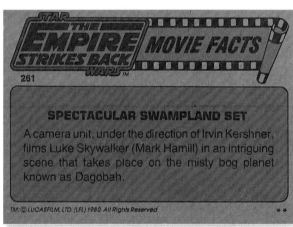

STAR WARS
THE EMPIRE STRIKES BACK™

MOVIE FACTS

261

SPECTACULAR SWAMPLAND SET

A camera unit, under the direction of Irvin Kershner, films Luke Skywalker (Mark Hamill) in an intriguing scene that takes place on the misty bog planet known as Dagobah.

ACTING CAN BE A DIRTY JOB!

MOVIE FACTS

262

ACTING CAN BE A DIRTY JOB!

Especially for poor R2-D2, who is tossed on shore by an annoyed swamp monster who has little taste for metal snacks. It all occurs on planet Dagobah, in a scene skilfully directed by Irvin Kershner.

**

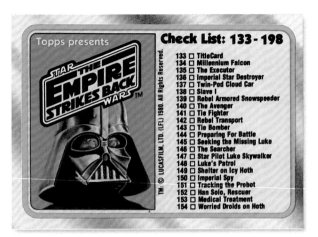

Topps presents

Check List: 133 - 198

133 ☐ Title Card
134 ☐ Millennium Falcon
135 ☐ The Executor
136 ☐ Imperial Star Destroyer
137 ☐ Twin-Pod Cloud Car
138 ☐ Slave I
139 ☐ Rebel Armored Snowspeeder
140 ☐ The Avenger
141 ☐ Tie Fighter
142 ☐ Rebel Transport
143 ☐ Tie Bomber
144 ☐ Preparing For Battle
145 ☐ Seeking the Missing Luke
146 ☐ The Searcher
147 ☐ Star Pilot Luke Skywalker
148 ☐ Luke's Patrol
149 ☐ Shelter on Icy Hoth
150 ☐ Imperial Spy
151 ☐ Tracking the Probot
152 ☐ Han Solo, Rescuer
153 ☐ Medical Treatment
154 ☐ Worried Droids on Hoth

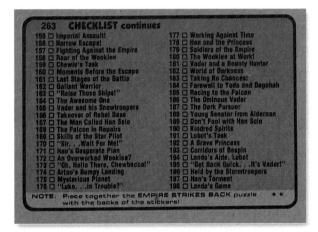

263 CHECKLIST continues

155 ☐ Imperial Assault!
156 ☐ Narrow Escape!
157 ☐ Fighting Against the Empire
158 ☐ Roar of the Wookiee
159 ☐ Chewie's Task
160 ☐ Moments Before the Escape
161 ☐ Last Stages of the Battle
162 ☐ Gallant Warrior
163 ☐ "Raise Those Ships!"
164 ☐ The Awesome One
165 ☐ Vader and his Snowtroopers
166 ☐ Takeover of Rebel Base
167 ☐ The Man Called Han Solo
168 ☐ The Falcon in Repairs
169 ☐ Skills of the Star Pilot
170 ☐ "Sir. . .Wait For Me!"
171 ☐ Han's Desperate Plan
172 ☐ An Overworked Wookiee?
173 ☐ "Oh, Hello There, Chewbacca!"
174 ☐ Artoo's Bumpy Landing
175 ☐ Mysterious Planet
176 ☐ "Luke. . .in Trouble?!"

177 ☐ Working Against Time
178 ☐ Han and the Princess
179 ☐ Soldiers of the Empire
180 ☐ The Wookiee at Work!
181 ☐ Vader and a Bounty Hunter
182 ☐ World of Darkness
183 ☐ Taking No Chances!
184 ☐ Farewell to Yoda and Dagobah
185 ☐ Racing to the Falcon
186 ☐ The Ominous Vader
187 ☐ The Dark Pursuer
188 ☐ Young Senator from Alderaan
189 ☐ Don't Fool with Han Solo
190 ☐ Kindred Spirits
191 ☐ Lobot's Task
192 ☐ A Brave Princess
193 ☐ Corridors of Bespin
194 ☐ Lando's Aide, Lobot
195 ☐ "Get Back Quick. . .It's Vader!"
196 ☐ Held by the Stormtroopers
197 ☐ Han's Torment
198 ☐ Lando's Game

NOTE: Piece together the EMPIRE STRIKES BACK puzzle ✶ ✶
with the backs of the stickers!

Topps presents

STAR THE EMPIRE STRIKES WARS™

Check List: 199 - 264

199 ☐ Deadly Device
200 ☐ In Vader's Clutches
201 ☐ A Tearful Farewell
202 ☐ Han Faces His Fate
203 ☐ Into The Carbon-Freezing Pit!
204 ☐ An Ugnaught
205 ☐ Tears of a Princess
206 ☐ Suspended in Carbon Freeze
207 ☐ Gruesome Fate!
208 ☐ Evil Threatens!
209 ☐ "This Deal is Getting Worse!"
210 ☐ The Captor, Boba Fett
211 ☐ Fear on Cloud City
212 ☐ A Warrior Driven
213 ☐ Courage of Skywalker
214 ☐ The Pursuer
215 ☐ Stalked by Vader!
216 ☐ A Droid Gone to Pieces
217 ☐ Threepio's Free Ride
218 ☐ Stormtrooper Takeover!
219 ☐ Princess Leia Under Guard!
220 ☐ Bounty Hunter Boba Fett

---

264 CHECKLIST continues

221 ☐ Lando Covers Their Escape!
222 ☐ Tumbling to an Unknown Fate
223 ☐ On the Verge of Defeat!
224 ☐ Gifted Performer
225 ☐ Actress Carrie Fisher
226 ☐ Han Solo (Harrison Ford)
227 ☐ Anthony Daniels as C-3PO
228 ☐ Our Favorite Protocol Droid
229 ☐ R2-D2 (Kenny Baker)
230 ☐ "Mynocks Outside? Oh My!"
231 ☐ Actor Billy Dee Williams
232 ☐ Galaxy's Most Loyal Droids
233 ☐ Dashing Han Solo
234 ☐ The Force and the Fury
235 ☐ Yoda's Squabble With R2-D2
236 ☐ Blasted by Leia!
237 ☐ The Art of Levitation
238 ☐ Snowswept Chewbacca
239 ☐ Dreamworld. . .Or Trap?
240 ☐ Swampland Peril!
241 ☐ "Tried, Have You?"
242 ☐ Encounter on Dagobah

243 ☐ Captain Solo Senses a Trap!
244 ☐ A Test For Luke
245 ☐ R2-D2 on the Misty Bog
246 ☐ Confronting the Dark Side
247 ☐ Luke Battles. . .Himself?
248 ☐ Blooming Romance
249 ☐ Chewie Retaliates
250 ☐ Stormtrooper Battle
251 ☐ Director Irvin Kershner
252 ☐ Spiffing Up a Wookiee
253 ☐ Filming The Falcon
254 ☐ Kershner Directs Mark Hamill
255 ☐ Shooting the Exciting Climax
256 ☐ Filming Vader in his Chamber
257 ☐ Dagobah Comes to Life
258 ☐ Building The Falcon
259 ☐ Hoth Rebel Base Sequence
260 ☐ Filming an Explosion
261 ☐ Spectacular Swampland Set
262 ☐ Acting Can be a Dirty Job!
263 ☐ Check List: 133 to 199
264 ☐ Check List: 200 to 264

NOTE. Piece together the EMPIRE STRIKES BACK puzzle ★ ★
with the backs of the stickers!

34 **

35 *

38 **

39 *

© LUCASFILM, LTD. (LFL) 1980. All Rights Reserved

© LUCASFILM, LTD. (LFL) 1980. All Rights Reserved

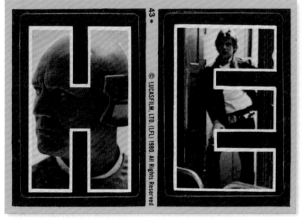

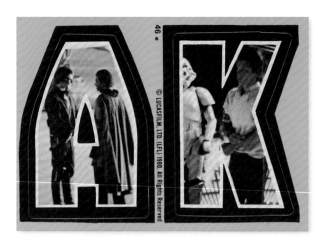

46 *

47 *

48 *

49 *

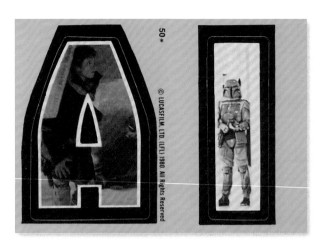

50*

51*

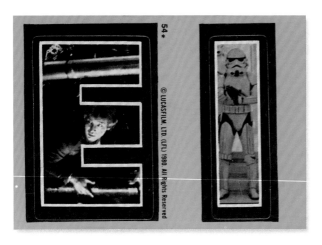

54 *

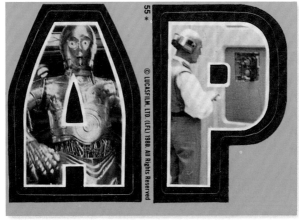

55 *

EMPIRE FORCES

DARTH VADER™

56

EMPIRE FORCES •

BOBA FETT™

57

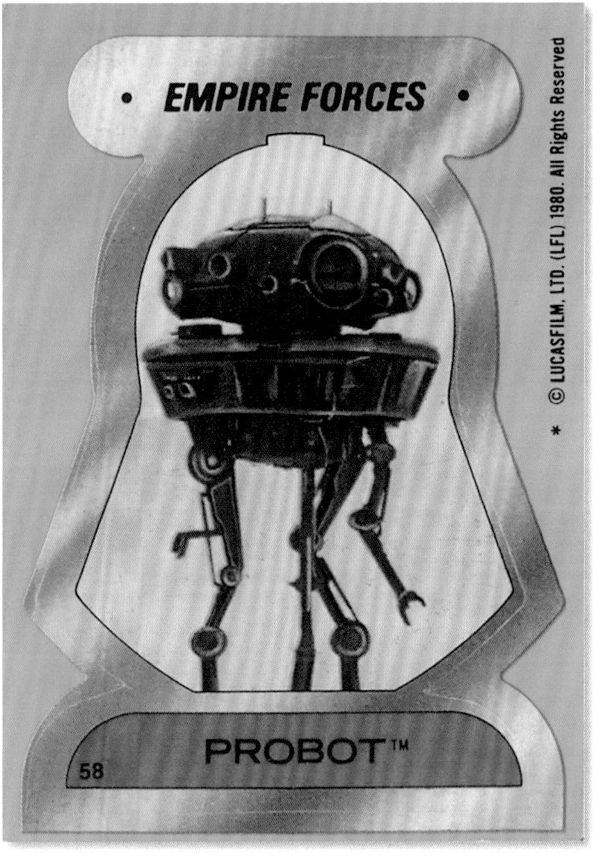

EMPIRE FORCES

PROBOT™

58

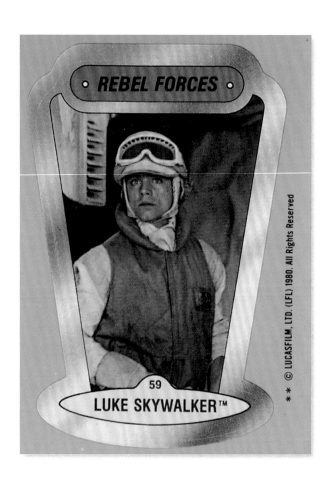

REBEL FORCES

© LUCASFILM, LTD. (LFL) 1980. All Rights Reserved

**

59

LUKE SKYWALKER™

REBEL FORCES

60
PRINCESS LEIA™

REBEL FORCES

62
LANDO CALRISSIAN™

REBEL FORCES

63
CHEWBACCA™

© LUCASFILM, LTD. (LFL) 1980. All Rights Reserved **

REBEL FORCES

64
R2-D2™

REBEL FORCES

66
YODA™

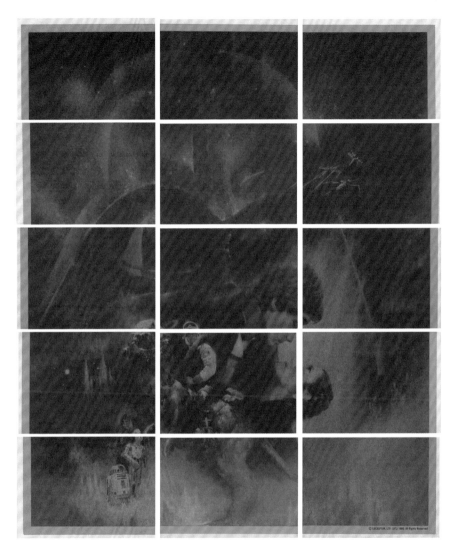

Roger Kastel's breathtaking artwork, seen here as the puzzle image for Series 2, was also used as the theatrical poster for *The Empire Strikes Back*.

We imposed a major color-scheme change for Series 3, with silver metallic backgrounds switched to gold and green outlines and captions replacing the previous red and blue. The outstretched hand of Darth Vader in our title card seems to beckon the buyer into taking one last, thankfully abbreviated visit to Hoth, Dagobah, Bespin, and points beyond. In a move that I recommended to management in order to curtail visual redundancy, we reduced the card number of our third and final *Empire* series to eighty-eight subjects, down from 132.

266

THE EMPIRE STRIKES BACK

STAR

"I cannot teach him, The boy has no patience."

QUOTES

Yoda to Ben Kenobi,
about Luke (EMPIRE)

**

Series 3 saw the return of character cards, complete with our distinctive Star File border design, only this time it was in comic book–style renderings, not photos. These exciting line illustrations were commissioned by Lucasfilm for the movie's release, which meant that we didn't receive them until the last minute. We also used the illustrations as design elements on the back of our oversized *The Empire Strikes Back* Photocards.

267

STAR WARS
THE EMPIRE STRIKES BACK ™

STAR

"With our combined strength we can end this destructive conflict and bring order to the galaxy."

QUOTES

Darth Vader to Luke (EMPIRE)

**

PRINCESS LEIA

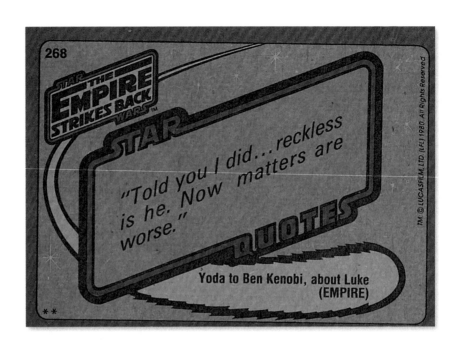

LUKE SKYWALKER

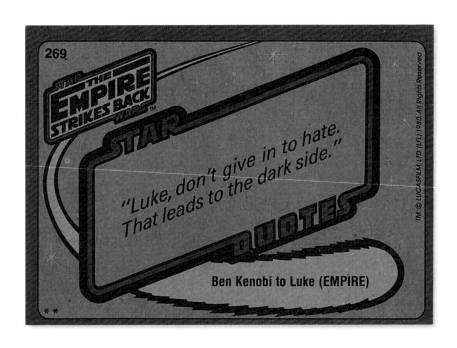

269

THE EMPIRE STRIKES BACK™

STAR

"*Luke, don't give in to hate. That leads to the dark side.*"

QUOTES

Ben Kenobi to Luke (EMPIRE)

C-3PO

270

"Oh my, what have you done!? I'm backwards!"

C-3PO to Chewbacca (EMPIRE)

**

R2-D2

DARTH VADER

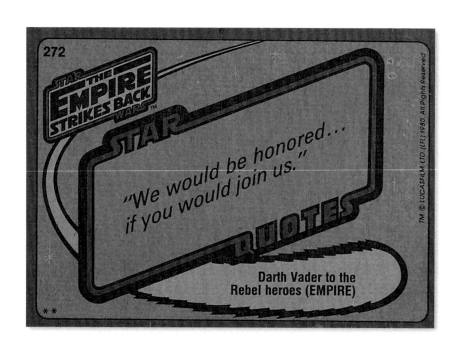

BOBA FETT

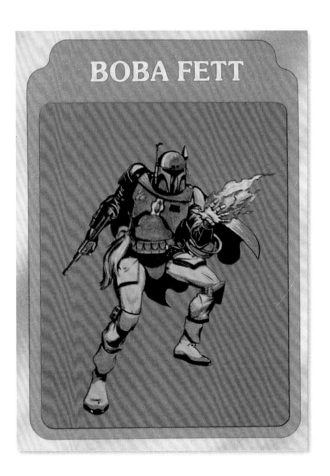

273

STAR WARS THE EMPIRE STRIKES BACK™

STAR QUOTES

"He's only a boy. But if he could be turned, he might become a powerful ally. He will join us or die, master."

Darth Vader to the Emperor (EMPIRE)

**

PROBOT

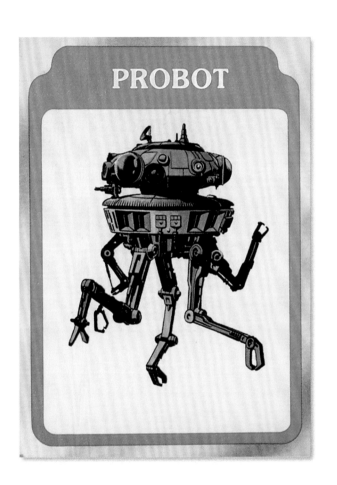

274

STAR

THE EMPIRE STRIKES BACK™

STAR

"The Force is with you, young Skywalker, but you are not a Jedi yet."

QUOTES

Darth Vader to Luke (EMPIRE)

**

DENGAR

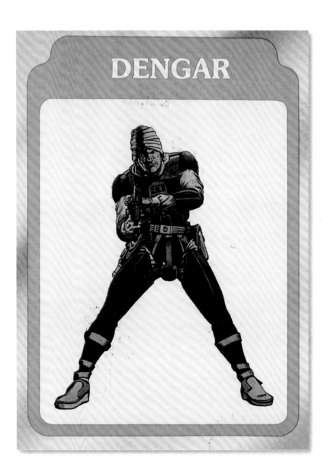

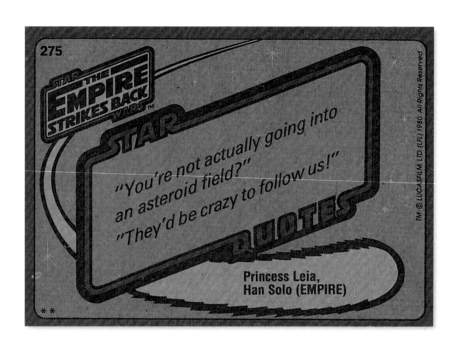

275

"You're not actually going into an asteroid field?"

"They'd be crazy to follow us!"

Princess Leia,
Han Solo (EMPIRE)

BOSSK

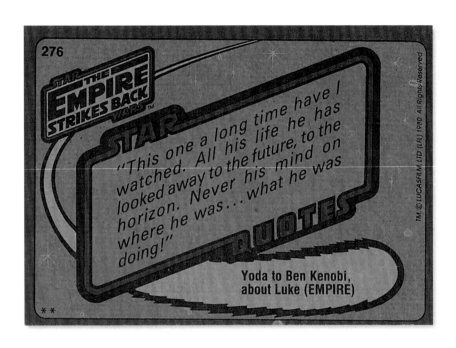

276

THE EMPIRE STRIKES BACK

STAR

"This one a long time have I watched. All his life he has looked away to the future, to the horizon. Never his mind on where he was... what he was doing!"

QUOTES

Yoda to Ben Kenobi, about Luke (EMPIRE)

* *

IG-88

FX-7

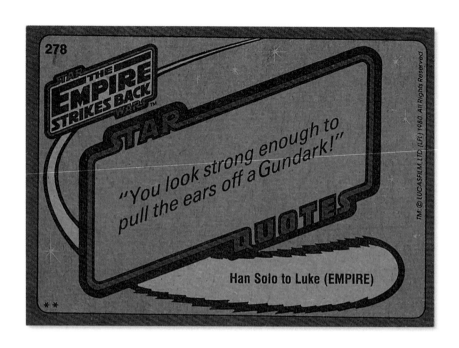

278

"You look strong enough to pull the ears off a Gundark!"

Han Solo to Luke (EMPIRE)

CHEWBACCA

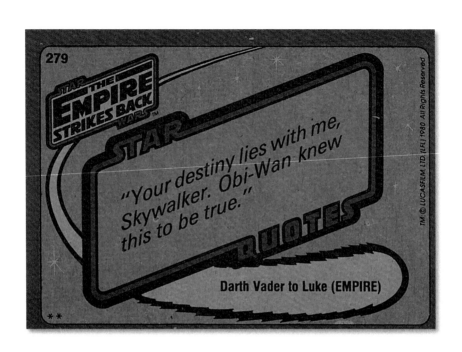

LANDO CALRISSIAN

STORMTROOPER

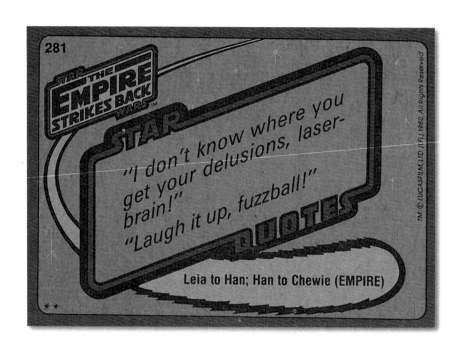

281

STAR WARS THE EMPIRE STRIKES BACK™

STAR

"I don't know where you get your delusions, laser-brain!"

"Laugh it up, fuzzball!"

QUOTES

Leia to Han; Han to Chewie (EMPIRE)

**

YODA

IMPERIAL SHIPS APPROACHING!

282

STAR THE EMPIRE STRIKES BACK WARS

STAR

"Mos Eisley Spaceport. You will never find a more wretched hive of scum and villainy. We must be cautious."

QUOTES

Ben Kenobi to Luke (STAR WARS)

THE COURAGEOUS TRENCH FIGHTERS!

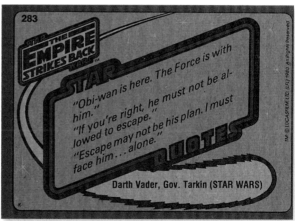

Another darkly realistic, *Paths of Glory*–like image, with a group of courageous soldiers facing impossible odds in the trenches.

284

THE EMPIRE STRIKES BACK™

STAR QUOTES

"Commander, tear this ship apart until you've found those plans and bring me the Ambassador. I want her alive!"

Darth Vader to Imperial Officer (STAR WARS)

TOO·ONEBEE

REBEL PROTOCOL DROIDS

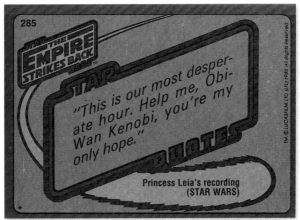

285

STAR THE EMPIRE STRIKES BACK WARS™

STAR

"This is our most desper-ate hour. Help me, Obi-Wan Kenobi, you're my only hope."

QUOTES

Princess Leia's recording
(STAR WARS)

TM © LUCASFILM LTD. (LFL) 1980. All Rights Reserved.

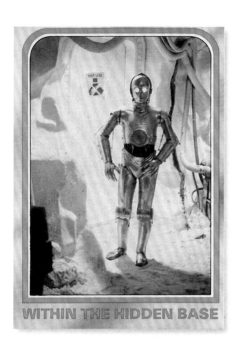

WITHIN THE HIDDEN BASE

286

STAR WARS THE EMPIRE STRIKES BACK

STAR QUOTES

"No light speed? It's not my fault!"

Han Solo to Princess Leia
(EMPIRE)

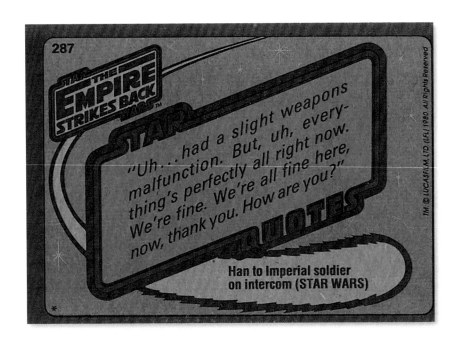

287

THE EMPIRE STRIKES BACK

"Uh... had a slight weapons malfunction. But, uh, everything's perfectly all right now. We're fine. We're all fine here, now, thank you. How are you?"

Han to Imperial soldier on intercom (STAR WARS)

CALRISSIAN OF BESPIN

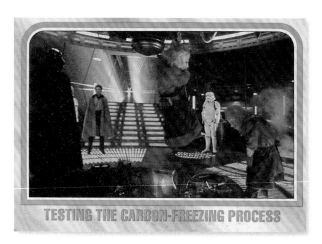

TESTING THE CARBON-FREEZING PROCESS

288

STAR WARS THE EMPIRE STRIKES BACK™

STAR

"Obi-Wan Kenobi…Obi-Wan? Now that's a name I haven't heard in a long time…a long time."

QUOTES

Ben Kenobi to Luke (STAR WARS)

FLIGHT OF THE X-WING

289

THE EMPIRE STRIKES BACK

STAR

"Between his howling and your blasting everything in sight, it's a wonder the whole station doesn't know we're here."

"Bring 'em on! I prefer a straight fight to all this sneaking around."

Luke, Han Solo (STAR WARS)

QUOTES

Luke heads for planet Dagobah after his rebel allies are routed on Hoth. As with the original *Star Wars*, we were given selected space-based shots only after the film was released, and even then in small quantities.

DODGING DEADLY LASERBLASTS!

290

THE EMPIRE STRIKES BACK

STAR

"Don't call me a mindless philosopher, you overweight glob of grease!"

QUOTES

C-3PO to R2-D2 (STAR WARS)

THE LOVERS PART

291

"I want to come with you to Alderaan. There's nothing here for me now. I want to learn the ways of the Force and become a Jedi like my father."

Luke to Ben Kenobi (STAR WARS)

This could easily have been captioned, "I LOVE YOU." "I KNOW."

CANYONS OF DEATH!

292

THE EMPIRE STRIKES BACK

STAR

"Ben...why didn't you tell me?"

QUOTES

Luke Skywalker (EMPIRE)

Now here's a really great money shot: the *Millennium Falcon* sweeps through the canyons of a giant asteroid as Imperial TIE fighters give chase. This was the exciting scene shown on network television in advance of the film's release, a clip eagerly watched by Len Brown and me (and half the nation, I imagine).

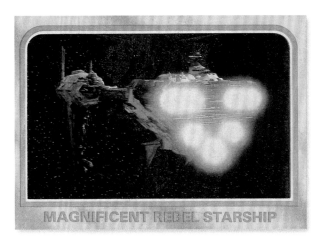

The final treat of *The Empire Strikes Back* is a view of the rebel fleet, comprised of various, previously unseen space vessels.

OLD FRIENDS. . . OR FOES?

294

STAR WARS: THE EMPIRE STRIKES BACK™

STAR QUOTES

"The regional governors now have direct control over territories. Fear will keep the local systems in line. Fear of this battle station."

Grand Moff Tarkin to Imperial generals (STAR WARS)

POWER OF THE EMPIRE

295

STAR THE
EMPIRE
STRIKES BACK
WARS™

STAR

"Governor Tarkin, I should have expected to find you holding Vader's leash. I recognized your foul stench when I was brought on board."

QUOTES

Princess Leia to Grand Moff Tarkin
(STAR WARS)

296

"Aren't you a little short for a stormtrooper?"

Princess Leia to Luke (STAR WARS)

THREEPIO IN A JAM!

SWAMP PLANET

297

STAR

EMPIRE
STRIKES BACK

"How did we get into this mess? I really don't know how. We seem to be made to suffer. It's our lot in life."

QUOTES

C-3PO to R2-D2 (STAR WARS)

A HASTY RETREAT!

298

THE EMPIRE STRIKES BACK™

STAR

"Did you hear that? They've shut down the main reactor. We'll be destroyed for sure. We're doomed!"

QUOTES

C-3PO to R2-D2 (STAR WARS)

299

THE
EMPIRE
STRIKES BACK

STAR

"Lando's not a system, he's a man. He's a gambler, scoundrel. You'd like him."

QUOTES

Han Solo to Princess Leia (EMPIRE)

HOSTILE WORLD OF HOTH

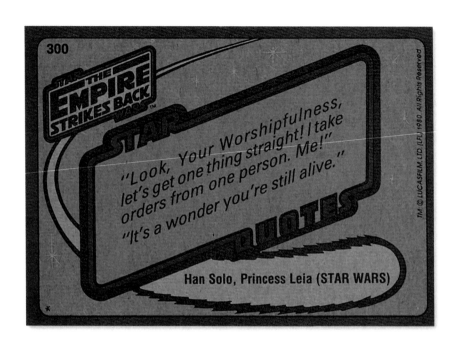

300

STAR WARS
THE EMPIRE
STRIKES BACK ™

STAR

"Look, Your Worshipfulness, let's get one thing straight! I take orders from one person. Me!"

"It's a wonder you're still alive."

Han Solo, Princess Leia (STAR WARS)

DESCENT INTO DANGER!

LUKE . . . LONG OVERDUE!

301

THE EMPIRE STRIKES BACK

STAR

"Your destiny lies along a different path from mine. The Force will be with you... always!"

QUOTES

Ben Kenobi to Luke (STAR WARS)

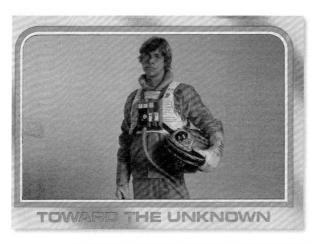

TOWARD THE UNKNOWN

302

EMPIRE
STRIKES BACK

"There's nothin' I can do about it, kid. I'm in full power. I'm going to have to shut down. But they're not gonna get me without a fight!"

Han Solo to Luke (STAR WARS)

For what it's worth, I stole this caption from an old 1950s William Holden movie, *Toward the Unknown*. This full shot of Luke Skywalker in his flight gear was part of an after-the-fact gallery session covering the main characters, which explains the blank background.

IN SEARCH OF HAN

303

THE EMPIRE STRIKES BACK™

TM © LUCASFILM LTD. (LFL) 1980 All Rights Reserved

"Luke's just not a farmer, Owen. He has too much of his father in him."

"That's what I'm afraid of."

Luke's Aunt Beru and
Uncle Owen (STAR WARS)

Here's a lovely galactic shot from the final scene of the movie, as Lando and Chewie take off to rescue carbon-frozen Han.

LUKE'S DESPERATE DECISION

304

STAR WARS
THE EMPIRE
STRIKES BACK™

"I've had just about enough of you! Go that way! You'll be malfunctioning within a day, you nearsighted scrap pile!"

C-3PO to R2-D2 (STAR WARS)

EMERGING FROM THE PIT

305

THE
EMPIRE
STRIKES BACK

STAR

"Wonderful girl! Either I'm going to kill her or I'm beginning to like her."

QUOTES

Han Solo to Luke (STAR WARS)

BUSY AS A WOOKIEE!

306

STAR WARS THE EMPIRE STRIKES BACK

STAR

"The Jedi are extinct, their fire has gone out of the universe. You, my friend, are all that's left of their religion."

QUOTES

Gov. Tarkin to Darth Vader
(STAR WARS)

307

THE EMPIRE STRIKES BACK

STAR QUOTES

"I sense something...a presence I haven't felt since...."

Darth Vader, speaking aloud to himself (STAR WARS)

PORTRAIT OF AN UGNAUGHT

THE WIZARD OF DAGOBAH

308

STAR *THE EMPIRE STRIKES BACK* *WARS*

TM © LUCASFILM LTD. (LFL) 1980. All Rights Reserved

STAR

"Afraid I was gonna leave without giving you a goodbye kiss?"
"I'd sooner kiss a Wookiee!"
"I can arrange that!"

QUOTES

Han Solo to Princess Leia (EMPIRE)

EMERGENCY REPAIRS!

309

STAR THE EMPIRE STRIKES BACK™

STAR QUOTES

"I find your lack of faith dis-turbing."

Darth Vader to Admiral Motti
(STAR WARS)

HAN ON THE ICY WASTELAND

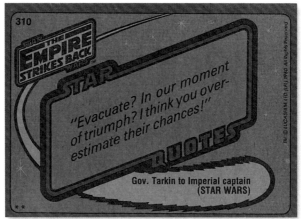

310

THE EMPIRE STRIKES BACK

STAR

"Evacuate? In our moment of triumph? I think you over-estimate their chances!"

QUOTES

Gov. Tarkin to Imperial captain
(STAR WARS)

THE WALKERS CLOSE IN!

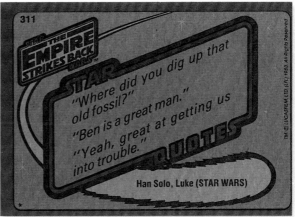

311

EMPIRE STRIKES BACK

STAR

"Where did you dig up that old fossil?"

"Ben is a great man."

"Yeah, great at getting us into trouble."

QUOTES

Han Solo, Luke (STAR WARS)

Any shot of the Imperial walkers was considered gold, so popular were the marching metal behemoths. This image is a mostly unaltered film frame, unlike many of the airbrushed visual effects images provided by Lucasfilm.

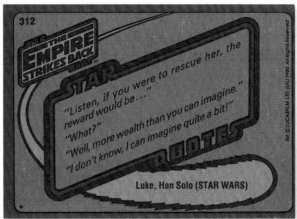

312

STAR WARS: THE EMPIRE STRIKES BACK

"Listen, if you were to rescue her, the reward would be…"

"What?"

"Well, more wealth than you can imagine."

"I don't know, I can imagine quite a bit!"

Luke, Han Solo (STAR WARS)

A beautiful FX composite image of the next-to-last shot in *Empire*. C-3PO and R2-D2 watch the *Falcon* depart on its rescue mission as recovered Luke comforts a heartbroken Leia, who tries her best to remain steadfast.

IN THE PATH OF DANGER!

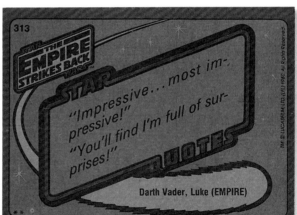

313

STAR THE EMPIRE STRIKES BACK

STAR QUOTES

"Impressive...most impressive!"
"You'll find I'm full of surprises!"

Darth Vader, Luke (EMPIRE)

THE X-WING COCKPIT

HERO OF THE REBELLION

315

THE EMPIRE STRIKES BACK

"For over a thousand genera-tions the Jedi Knights were the guardians of peace and justice in the Old Republic. Before the dark times, before the Empire."

Ben Kenobi to Luke (STAR WARS)

TM © LUCASFILM LTD. (LFL) 1980 All Rights Reserved

VADER'S PRIVATE CHAMBER

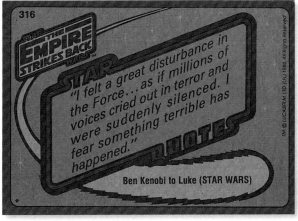

316

STAR THE EMPIRE STRIKES BACK WARS

STAR

"I felt a great disturbance in the Force... as if millions of voices cried out in terror and were suddenly silenced. I fear something terrible has happened."

QUOTES

Ben Kenobi to Luke (STAR WARS)

ABOARD THE EXECUTOR

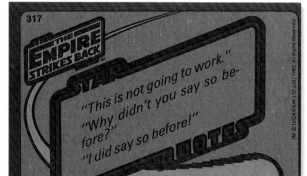

317

THE EMPIRE STRIKES BACK

STAR

"This is not going to work."
"Why didn't you say so be-fore?"
"I did say so before!"

QUOTES

Luke, Han Solo (STAR WARS)

TM © LUCASFILM LTD. (LFL) 1980. All Rights Reserved

THE OMINOUS ONE

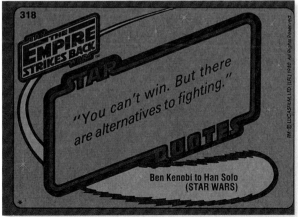

318

STAR WARS THE EMPIRE STRIKES BACK™

STAR

"You can't win. But there are alternatives to fighting."

QUOTES

Ben Kenobi to Han Solo
(STAR WARS)

LORD VADER'S ORDERS

319

THE EMPIRE STRIKES BACK

STAR WARS QUOTES

"Dantooine is too remote to make an effective demonstration. But don't worry. We will deal with your Rebel friends soon enough."

Gov. Tarkin to Princess Leia
(STAR WARS)

TM & © LUCASFILM LTD (LFL) 1980. All Rights Reserved

"HE'S STILL ALIVE!"

320

THE EMPIRE STRIKES BACK

STAR

"I am altering the deal. Pray that I don't alter it any further."

QUOTES

Darth Vader to Lando (EMPIRE)

LANDO'S WARM RECEPTION

321

STAR

THE
EMPIRE
STRIKES BACK™

"Don't be too proud of this technological terror you've constructed. The ability to destroy a
planet is insignificant next to the
power of the Force."

QUOTES

Darth Vader to
Imperial generals (STAR WARS)

THE LANDING

322

EMPIRE STRIKES BACK

STAR

"The Force is what gives the Jedi his power. It's an energy field created by all living things. It surrounds us and penetrates us. It binds the galaxy together."

QUOTES

Ben Kenobi to Luke (STAR WARS)

Another unairbrushed film frame enabled us to showcase ILM's matte painting of Cloud City—a vista later digitally enhanced for Lucas's *Star Wars Trilogy: Special Edition* in 1997.

323

"Who's the more foolish... the fool or the fool who follows him?"

Ben Kenobi to Han Solo (STAR WARS)

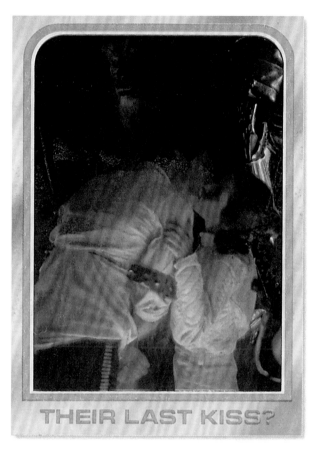

THEIR LAST KISS?

Nice smooch!

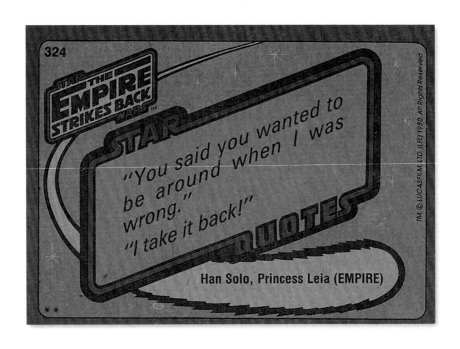

324

"You said you wanted to be around when I was wrong."
"I take it back!"

Han Solo, Princess Leia (EMPIRE)

BOUNTY HUNTER IG-88

THE ICY PLAINS OF HOTH

325

STAR THE EMPIRE STRIKES BACK WARS™

STAR

"Don't worry, she'll hold together. You hear me, baby? Hold together!!"

QUOTES

Han to Luke, Han
to his ship (STAR WARS)

TM © LUCASFILM LTD. (LFL) 1980. All Rights Reserved.

LUKE ASTRIDE HIS TAUNTAUN

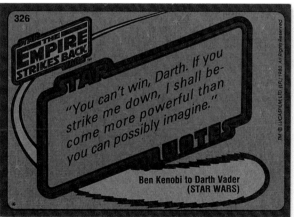

326

"You can't win, Darth. If you strike me down, I shall become more powerful than you can possibly imagine."

Ben Kenobi to Darth Vader
(STAR WARS)

Luke astride his tauntaun appears at the very beginning of the movie. We eventually reused it as one of our deluxe, oversized *Empire* Photocards (page 527).

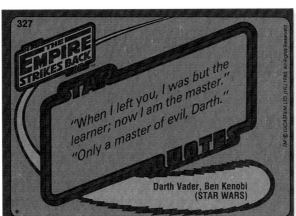

A tad overairbrushed but gorgeous nonetheless: Rebel fighters square off against behemoth-like Imperial walkers on Hoth. Back in the day, I would have killed for a few more images such as this.

CHAMPIONS OF FREEDOM

This flattering group shot of *Empire*'s rebel heroes was so strong we reused it as an oversized Photocard (page 545).

329

THE EMPIRE STRIKES BACK

STAR

"Hokey religions and an-cient weapons are no match for a good blaster at your side, kid."

QUOTES

Han Solo to Luke (STAR WARS)

INSIDE THE FALCON

330

THE EMPIRE STRIKES BACK

"Got him! I got him!"
"Great, kid! Don't get cocky."

Luke, Han Solo (STAR WARS)

THE TRAINING OF A JEDI

YODA'S INSTRUCTION

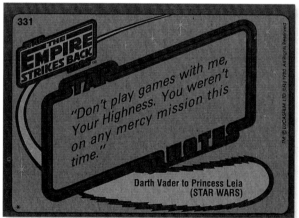

331

STAR THE EMPIRE STRIKES BACK TM

"Don't play games with me, Your Highness. You weren't on any mercy mission this time."

Darth Vader to Princess Leia
(STAR WARS)

TM © LUCASFILM LTD. (LFL) 1980. All Rights Reserved

THE WARRIOR AND THE JEDI MASTER

332

"Look, I ain't in this for your revolution, and I'm not in it for you, Princess. I expect to be well paid. I'm in it for the money!"

Han Solo to Princess Leia (STAR WARS)

A dramatic and iconic image of the menacing Imperial walkers marching inexorably toward a mostly one-sided confrontation with rebel forces.

THE ASTEROID CHASE

334

"Oh, my! Artoo! You must repair him! Sir, if any of my circuits or gears will help, I'll gladly donate them."

C-3PO, regarding Artoo (STAR WARS)

It's hard to tell where the photo ends and Lucasfilm's retouching begins, but this image does impressively capture the adrenaline-pumping excitement of Han's desperate flight through an asteroid field as he skillfully dodges blasts from pursuing X-wings. This image also serves as a puzzle for the sticker backs (pages 510–11).

APPROACHING PLANET DAGOBAH

335

"Oh! The garbage chute was a really wonderful idea. What an incredible smell you've discovered!"

Han Solo to Princess Leia
(STAR WARS)

Another subset idea from Series 1 was called on for Series 3: "Space Paintings," which offer a second round of artist Ralph McQuarrie's exquisite preproduction renderings.

SPACE PAINTINGS
by RALPH McQUARRIE

BEAUTY OF BESPIN

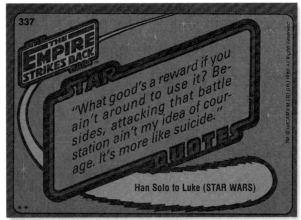

337

"What good's a reward if you ain't around to use it? Besides, attacking that battle station ain't my idea of courage. It's more like suicide."

Han Solo to Luke (STAR WARS)

SPACE PAINTINGS
by RALPH McQUARRIE

DREAMLIKE CITY

338

THE EMPIRE STRIKES BACK

STAR QUOTES

"I knew you'd come back. I just knew it!"
"Well, I wasn't gonna let you get all the credit and take all the reward!"

Luke, Han Solo (STAR WARS)

SPACE PAINTINGS
by RALPH McQUARRIE

LUKE'S TRAINING

339

"Still, she's got a lot of spirit. I don't know, what do you think? Do you think a princess and a guy like me..."
"No!"

Han Solo, Luke (STAR WARS)

SPACE PAINTINGS

by RALPH McQUARRIE

SNOW WALKER TERROR

340

THE EMPIRE STRIKES BACK

"You're all clear, kid. Now let's blow this thing and go home!"

Han Solo to Luke (STAR WARS)

SPACE PAINTINGS
by RALPH McQUARRIE

TAUNTAUN

341

THE EMPIRE STRIKES BACK

STAR QUOTES

"The Force is strong with this one!"

Darth Vader, while chasing Luke
(STAR WARS)

SPACE PAINTINGS
by RALPH McQUARRIE

CLOUD CITY REACTOR·SHAFT

342

"Together we will rule the galaxy, father and son. Luke...it is your destiny!"

Darth Vader to Luke (EMPIRE)

SPACE PAINTINGS
by RALPH McQUARRIE

YODA'S HOME

343

EMPIRE
STRIKES BACK
STAR WARS

STAR

"This will be a day long re-membered. It has seen the end of Kenobi and will soon see the end of the Rebellion."

QUOTES

Darth Vader to Gov. Tarkin
(STAR WARS)

SPACE PAINTINGS
by RALPH McQUARRIE

ESCAPE FROM BESPIN

344

"Great shot, kid. That was one in a million!"

Han Solo to Luke (STAR WARS)

SPACE PAINTINGS
by RALPH McQUARRIE

DEADLY STOMPERS

345

THE EMPIRE STRIKES BACK

STAR

"At least you're still in one piece. Look what happened to me!"

QUOTES

C-3PO to R2-D2 (EMPIRE)

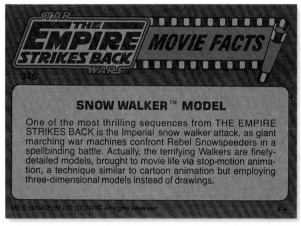

Our final subset in this series is a small group of behind-the-scenes Movie Facts cards. I remember having fun designing a film strip–style graphic, complete with sprockets, as the holding device for the captions and text.

OF HELMETS AND COSTUMES

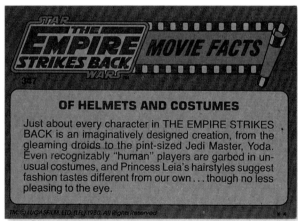

347

OF HELMETS AND COSTUMES

Just about every character in THE EMPIRE STRIKES BACK is an imaginatively designed creation, from the gleaming droids to the pint-sized Jedi Master, Yoda. Even recognizably "human" players are garbed in unusual costumes, and Princess Leia's hairstyles suggest fashion tastes different from our own . . . though no less pleasing to the eye.

FILMING THE STAR DESTROYER

MOVIE FACTS

348

FILMING THE STAR DESTROYER™

The Imperial Star Destroyer, massive spacecraft first introduced in STAR WARS, is seen quite a lot in THE EMPIRE STRIKES BACK. The ship in reality is a large-sized model crafted by the special effects technicians at Industrial Light and Magic.

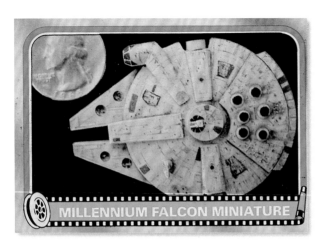

MILLENNIUM FALCON MINIATURE

STAR WARS THE EMPIRE STRIKES BACK — MOVIE FACTS

349

MILLENNIUM FALCON™ MINIATURE

Han Solo's saucer-shaped pirateship *Millennium Falcon* is once again in the thick of things as THE EMPIRE STRIKES BACK continues the explosive STAR WARS saga. Many models were used during the course of the film, all varying in size. Here, to scale, is one of the tinier models.

**

LAUNCHING AN X-WING

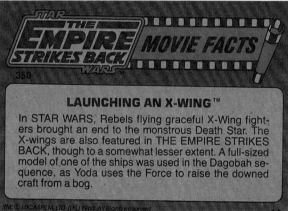

STAR WARS
THE EMPIRE STRIKES BACK

MOVIE FACTS

350

LAUNCHING AN X-WING™

In STAR WARS, Rebels flying graceful X-Wing fighters brought an end to the monstrous Death Star. The X-wings are also featured in THE EMPIRE STRIKES BACK, though to a somewhat lesser extent. A full-sized model of one of the ships was used in the Dagobah sequence, as Yoda uses the Force to raise the downed craft from a bog.

STAR DESTROYER™ IN POSITION

There are many stars in the STAR WARS movies . . .
movie stars to be sure, though not all of them are actors.
The costume designers, painters, special effects wizards and model makers are essential to a motion picture
of this kind, and all strive to dazzle viewers with new and
more exciting creations.

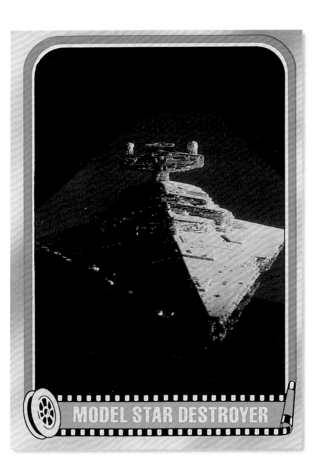

MODEL STAR DESTROYER

CHECKLIST

STAR THE EMPIRE STRIKES BACK WARS ™

265 to 352

265 ☐ Title Card
266 ☐ Art: Han Solo
267 ☐ Art: Princess Leia
268 ☐ Art: Luke Skywalker
269 ☐ Art: C-3PO
270 ☐ Art: R2-D2
271 ☐ Art: Darth Vader
272 ☐ Art: Boba Fett
273 ☐ Art: Probot
274 ☐ Art: Dengar
275 ☐ Art: Bossk
276 ☐ Art: IG-88

277 ☐ Art: FX-7
278 ☐ Art: Chewbacca
279 ☐ Art: Lando Calrissian
280 ☐ Art: Stormtrooper
281 ☐ Art: Yoda
282 ☐ Imperial Ships Approaching!
283 ☐ The Courageous Trench Fighters!
284 ☐ Too-Onebee
285 ☐ Rebel Protocol Droids
286 ☐ Within The Hidden Base
287 ☐ Calrissian Of Bespin
288 ☐ Testing The Carbon-Freezing Process
289 ☐ Flight of the X-Wing
290 ☐ Dodging Deadly Laserblasts!
291 ☐ The Lovers Part
292 ☐ Canyons of Death!
293 ☐ Magnificent Rebel Starship
294 ☐ Old Friends . . . Or Foes?
295 ☐ Power of the Empire
296 ☐ Threepio In a Jam!
297 ☐ Swamp Planet
298 ☐ A Hasty Retreat!
299 ☐ Hostile World of Hoth
300 ☐ Descent Into Danger!
301 ☐ Luke . . . Long Overdue!
302 ☐ Toward The Unknown

352

303 ☐ In Search of Han
304 ☐ Luke's Desperate Decision
305 ☐ Emerging From The Pit
306 ☐ Busy as a Wookiee!
307 ☐ Portrait of an Ugnaught
308 ☐ The Wizard of Dagobah
309 ☐ Emergency Repairs!
310 ☐ Han on the Icy Wasteland
311 ☐ The Walkers Close In!
312 ☐ Toward Tomorrow . . .
313 ☐ In the Path of Danger!
314 ☐ The X-Wing Cockpit
315 ☐ Hero of the Rebellion
316 ☐ Vader's Private Chamber
317 ☐ Aboard the Executor
318 ☐ The Ominous One
319 ☐ Lord Vader's Orders
320 ☐ "He's Still Alive!"
321 ☐ Lando's Warm Reception
322 ☐ The Landing
323 ☐ Their Last Kiss?
324 ☐ Bounty Hunter IG-88
325 ☐ The Icy Plains of Hoth
326 ☐ Luke Astride His Tauntaun
327 ☐ Rebel Snowspeeders Zero In!

328 ☐ Champions of Freedom
329 ☐ Inside the Falcon
330 ☐ The Training of a Jedi
331 ☐ Yoda's Instruction
332 ☐ The Warrior and the Jedi Master
333 ☐ Imperial Snow Walker Attack!
334 ☐ The Asteroid Chase
335 ☐ Approaching Planet Dagobah
336 ☐ Painting: Power Generators
337 ☐ Painting: Beauty of Bespin
338 ☐ Painting: Dreamlike City
339 ☐ Painting: Luke's Training
340 ☐ Painting: Snow Walker Terror
341 ☐ Painting: Tauntaun
342 ☐ Painting: Cloud City Reactor Shaft
343 ☐ Painting: Yoda's Home
344 ☐ Painting: Escape From Bespin
345 ☐ Painting: Deadly Stompers
346 ☐ Snow Walker Model
347 ☐ Of Helmets and Costumes
348 ☐ Filming the Star Destroyer
349 ☐ Millennium Falcon Miniature
350 ☐ Launching An X-Wing
351 ☐ Model Star Destroyer
352 ☐ Checklist

NOTE: Piece together the EMPIRE STRIKES BACK puzzle with the backs of the stickers! ✶ ✶

67 * *

68 *

69 *

70 **

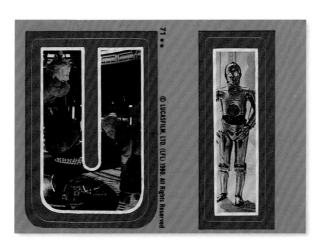

71 **

72 **

73 ★

74 ★★

77 **

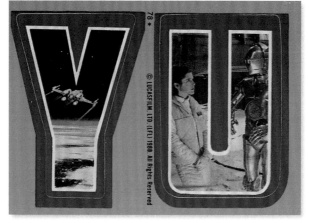

78 *

79 *

80 *

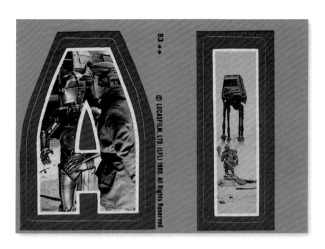

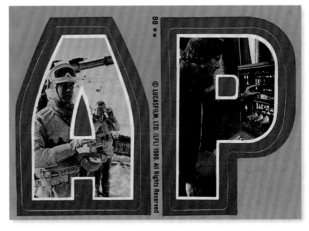

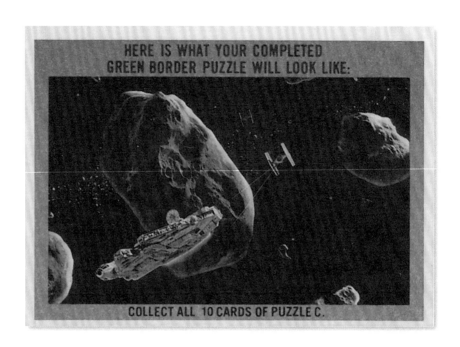

HERE IS WHAT YOUR COMPLETED
GREEN BORDER PUZZLE WILL LOOK LIKE:

COLLECT ALL 10 CARDS OF PUZZLE C.

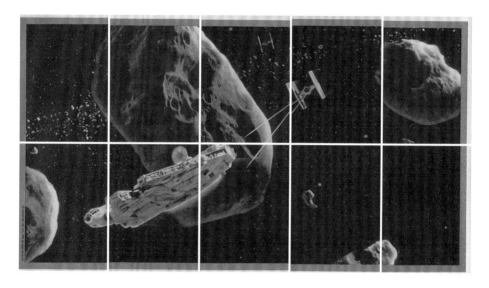

The *Millennium Falcon* evades a fleet of TIE fighters by heading into an asteroid field in this exciting promotional image supplied by the studio.

In this final puzzle, a pensive Yoda trains Luke in the ways of the Force on Dagobah.

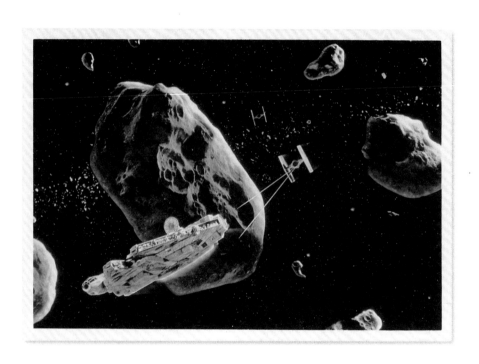

topps® STAR WARS THE EMPIRE STRIKES BACK

PHOTO CARDS

CHECKLIST

#1

SEE CHECKLIST #2 FOR #16 TO #30

1 ☐   2 ☐   3 ☐

4 ☐   5 ☐   6 ☐

7 ☐   8 ☐   9 ☐

10 ☐   11 ☐   12 ☐

13 ☐   14 ☐   15 ☐

3-4-26-06-01-0

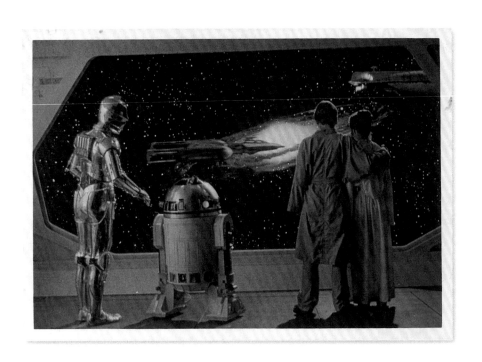

PHOTO CARDS

CHECKLIST #2

SEE CHECKLIST #1 FOR #1 TO #15

16 ☐

17 ☐   18 ☐   19 ☐

20 ☐   21 ☐   22 ☐

23 ☐   24 ☐   25 ☐   26 ☐

27 ☐   28 ☐   29 ☐   30 ☐

THE OFFICIAL STAR WARS™ FAN CLUB

What you get: Quarterly Newsletter + THE EMPIRE STRIKES BACK™ new membership kit which includes SWFC poster.

To join: Send your name, address, and a check or money order for $5.00 ($6.00 in Canada) to:

Star Wars Fan Club • P.O. Box 8905 — Dept. B3 • Universal City, CA 91608

Please do not send cash.

Allow 4-6 weeks for delivery of membership kit.

GIANT
FULL COLOR PHOTOCARDS

THE EMPIRE STRIKES BACK™

TOPPS CHEWING GUM, INC., DURYEA, PA. 18642

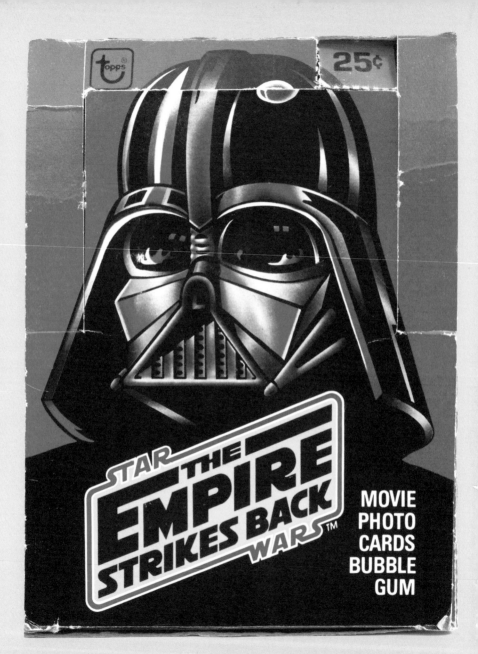